1

This book is lovingly dedicated
to the memory of my parents,
Bill and Florence Popoff.

By example, you taught me
the importance of the Doukhobor creed
"Toil and Peaceful Life".

TABLE OF CONTENTS

FORWARD

Written by Betty White

The story of Thelma Yuille's life, covered briefly in these pages, is an inspiration. I have only known Thelma since we met in Logan Lake, B.C. I am Betty White, wife of the Reverend Godfrey White mentioned in this book. Yes, we were definitely elderly when we met a young Thelma.

Thelma reminds me of what our Lord said about Nathaniel: "He found him to be a man in whom there was no guile." John 1:45-49, KJV. Thelma, in her writing, as in her life, tells it as she 'experienced' the various episodes. It is difficult for her to bare her soul, but knowing the Spirit was leading her to write and share her experiences and testimony, she has been guided by the Lord Jesus and the Holy Spirit.

Thelma looks on me as a mentor, friend, and sister in the Lord. She has been to me a blessing, an inspiration, and an example of unwavering faith during some very difficult times on her journey.

Thelma, after my beloved husband went to be with the Lord in 1995, has taken me driving in her little pink four wheel drive vehicle to the ski trails, creeks, and back woods of Logan Lake. She has introduced me to the nature I love, as seen through her eyes. As we let our dogs run, we travelled at about 5 kilometers an hour. Wildlife was in abundance, including deer, bear, moose, plants, nests, hollow logs, and streams. How we rejoiced in our fellowship.

May this little book be an inspiration and challenge to many. Thank-you Thelma, and to God be the glory for showing you the way.

PREFACE

Every single person has a story to tell. This is mine.

I can honestly say that I never intended to write a book, and certainly not one about my rather ordinary life. However, recently I have felt very strongly inspired to record specific incidents that have happened to me, and put them together in a book. This is that book.

I grew up firmly believing that there were two kinds of people in this world, the 'us' and the 'them'. There were those who worked hard, had our feet on the ground, and lived a regular, normal life, the 'us'. There were very many of us in the Swan River Valley in rural Saskatchewan/Manitoba. Speaking strictly for myself, I was comfortable in the knowledge that God was in heaven, where He belonged, and we were on earth, where we belonged, and everything and everyone was exactly where they should be. Because there is power in numbers and I belonged to the population majority in our family's social circle, this made my belief system unquestionably right.

However, there were also 'them' in our midst. They, too, worked hard, and even looked and seemed like regular, normal folk for the most part, *but* they willingly and voluntarily went to church once a week, prayed to, kneeled before, and even sang special songs about *'their'* God! If that wasn't bad enough, they would talk to each other and maybe even sometimes mention something to 'us' about their God randomly, at any old time, if given an opportunity to do so. They didn't even wait until Sunday! I found this to be rather unnerving.

Seriously, what was wrong with them?

I had a firm notion that this different belief system of theirs was certainly something I needed to be extremely wary of, simply because there is fear associated with the unknown.

Even though I knew very little about Christianity, I felt that God was very special. God was to be revered, put high up on a pedestal, maybe even worshipped somehow, but certainly unapproachable by just anybody. Not only that, surely there must be a ritual of some sort that a person would have to perform in order to get His attention, although I had absolutely no idea in the world as to why anyone would even feel the need to do so.

When I was thirty-four years old, devastated by suddenly losing my father to cancer, a divine, surreal experience changed my life in seconds. The heavens opened wide, right before my very eyes, and for a few brief seconds, I experienced the majestic power of God's unconditional love flow freely throughout my soul to the absolute and very core of my being. Physically, I was standing with my feet planted firmly on earth. Spiritually, I was clearly and definitely united with and blissfully at one with God and Jesus in the heavenly realm.

As the chapters of this book unfolded while I merely wrote down some personal experiences, I was able to see how all they fit together perfectly to bring me to where I am today. The story is not told in a strictly chronological order. Some instances are recorded together because they relate to a specific topic.

Throughout the book, in a different font, are scripture readings quoted directly from the New Living Translation Bible. I feel they relate directly to the circumstances that I was experiencing in my life at the time, even though I had absolutely no knowledge of the written word in the Bible at any point in my younger years. These quotations, however, confirm to me that even at a time in my life when I did not know God or Jesus or the Holy Spirit, they were quietly but actively at work in my life.

At the back of the book is a section "Bible Study Notes", which explains in more detail each ancient scripture reading that I have chosen to use. To me, these explanations are proof that God's Word still relates directly to us today. They not only confirm that God is ultimately at work in each of our lives daily, but also that there is a time, a place, and a reason for everything that happens to each and every one of us.

Even though many events recorded here involve my entire family, the main focus is on my own personal journey. All recorded incidents are strictly from my own point of view, and I take full responsibility for everything that is written. Although my husband's beliefs are different from mine, he has agreed to be mentioned in the instances which involve him directly that I have written about here.

It has been an interesting journey, and one I hope you will enjoy reading about.

Chapter 1

Roots

I grew up on a small farm in Saskatchewan, one mile from the Manitoba border, in what was primarily a Doukhobor rural community. The nearest town was Benito, Manitoba, approximately ten miles away. Our farm was located near the southern base of Thunder Hill in the Swan River Valley.

For those unfamiliar with Doukhobors, here is an extremely simplistic explanation: in the 18th century, some Russian peasants began to split away from the authoritative practices, affluence and elaborate rituals of the Russian Orthodox Church. They decided instead to accept a more simplistic faith by recognizing the spirit of God in every individual and trusting themselves to look within to hear the voice of God. Consequently, they did not accept the need for institutionalized priesthood or clergy. Threatened by this movement, the Church and Czarist authorities persecuted the peasants for over two hundred years. On June 29, 1895 approximately seven thousand Russian peasants took a collective stand for peace and burned all their guns, refusing to kill another human being, honoring the commandment, 'Thou Shalt Not Kill'. For this act of defiance against Czarist authorities, the Doukhobors were beaten, tortured, and their freedom stripped away. The survivors were exiled and marched into northern Siberia and held in detention under extremely harsh conditions. Their suffering and oppression received world-wide attention from Protestants with pacifistic ideals, the Quakers in England and America, and Leo Tolstoy, a famous Russian novelist. The Czar of Russia, Nicolas 11, granted a reprieve permitting them to emigrate to Canada, a land where they could practice ideals of non-violence and pacifism, living free of oppression. They settled in Saskatchewan, which was, at the time, the barren Northwest Territories. By 1907, the majority had moved to British Columbia.

By the time I came into this world, the hardships endured by my ancestors were passed on as stories to the younger generations. I was second oldest of six children. We were a very close family, and fortunate enough to have three generations living in the same farmyard. My siblings and I are third generation Canadians. We grew up speaking fluent Russian. I specifically remember my father telling my mother one day that they should start speaking in English once in a while at home, so that us kids would know at least some English when we started school. My grandparents (my father's mother and father) lived in their own house, only several feet away from ours. My other grandparents lived about 20 miles away in the town of Pelly, Saskatchewan. They had been born and raised on farms in that area, and had moved off the farm and into town in their elder years. Our families visited back and forth very regularly. I remember growing up feeling very content and thinking that I knew exactly who I was and where I belonged, in this close, Doukhobor family.

Like pretty much everyone else in the immediate farming area, we owned horses and raised cows, pigs, chickens, and sometimes ducks or turkeys for our own use. One year my parents raised geese, but they were unpredictable and very aggressive, often chasing the younger and smaller kids around in the yard. We always had a huge vegetable garden which provided vegetables for our entire family for a year. Our mother canned homegrown peas, beans, corn, beets, and carrots for the winter months. Cabbage was generally made into sauerkraut for keeping throughout the winter. Others vegetables, like lettuce, spinach, radish, watermelon and pumpkin were enjoyed fresh during the summer months while they were in season. Onions and garlic were hung to dry for winter use. Mountains of potatoes were dug up in the fall and stored in the cellar along with root vegetables until the next crop was ready the next fall. There was no electricity in our area, so freezing food was not an option. Always, every single year, we would plant row upon row of sunflowers. The seeds were harvested, dried in the sun, and stored in sacks to enjoy all winter long. Doukhobors are very well known for their love of sunflower seeds. This was long before 'spitz' ever became popular. Spitz is a brand name of sunflower seeds now available commercially.

When the berries were ripe, we would go in groups to pick wild raspberries, wild strawberries, and wild blueberries. My sisters and I were each given a little tin can tied by a rope around our waist. The idea was to fill our little cans with berries then dump them into my mothers or grandmothers bucket. I'm sure that I ate more than what I ever put into the little tin can but it kept my sisters and I busy. If I donated even one little handful of berries that I could not manage to eat, I figured this warranted enjoying a huge portion of dessert because I had 'helped'! My mother would bake the absolutely most delicious sweet perohy with the fresh berries. Sweet perohy are a traditional Russian dessert, somewhat like individual tarts that were eaten with fresh or sour cream. Sometimes she would make regular pies. Much of the fruit was also made into jam or canned in quarts so that we would have fruit in the winter time.

There was never a lack of work to do on the farm. My father and my mother, my grandfather and my grandmother, and whichever any of the kids who were old enough to be more of a help than a hindrance at the time, had specific chores to tend to. Winter and summer, clothes were washed in what are now antique washing machines and hung out on clotheslines to dry (or freeze solid). Water was hauled up from the well by the pail full. One job that did seem to fall specifically towards the older kids was carrying wood from outside to fill the wood box for the wood burning stove, winter and summer. We could also pick stones in the fields with relative ease, considering our proximity to the ground, and I remember spending very many days at that particular task. One field especially had so many stones that it affected the yield of harvest.

At harvest time, the Doukhobor men all got together and worked together in threshing crews, travelling from one farm to the next, until everyone's wheat harvest was in. In my youth, we owned tractors to work the fields, but I remember my grandfather telling stories about working with oxen and horses.

Doukhobors love to sing, and no gathering of family and friends was complete without an enthusiastic sing along being rendered in beautiful and perfect harmony by everyone present. They just seemed to do it effortlessly, no matter who was present. My grandmother had an old, Russian songbook that was a very treasured object in their home. My mother and father were both musically talented. They both belonged to a band called the 'Riverside Ramblers', and played at many weddings and barn dances before we children came along. My father played the guitar, mandolin, violin, banjo, and also sang. My mother played the accordion. As the family grew and their commitments to wee ones took up most of their precious free time, they stopped playing publically. On many warm, summer weekends, however, neighbors would come over after evening chores were done, bringing their guitars, fiddles, and voices for an evening of music and entertainment. Our little log farm house was too small to accommodate everyone inside, so the adults would simply go outdoors and build a huge campfire (from our massive woodpile) and sit around on chairs or logs, often partying into the wee hours, long after us kids went to bed.

Once a year on June 29, Doukhobors in our rural area travelled to Veregin, Sask. to celebrate St. Peter's Day. In Canada, these celebrations included songs, stories, and speeches. There was always plenty of traditional food at this yearly gathering, and families enjoyed seeing loved ones from other villages whom they had not seen for months.

The Russian Orthodox Church still follows the old Julian calendar, and therefore Christmas day in the old country has always been celebrated on January 7. When Christmas in Canada was celebrated on December 25, our grandparents gently reminded us that the real Christmas is on January 7. They reminded us again on January 7 that 'today is the *real* Christmas'.

Our social network consisted almost strictly of Doukhobors, and Sundays were often spent visiting friends and relatives. Whenever the "old people" got together, stories from generations past were always told amongst themselves and to the children, too, if we chose to stick around and listen. Many of these stories were about life in the 'old country', and loved ones left behind. Other stories related to very harsh living conditions upon arriving in a new country, and the strangeness of everything in this new land. I loved listening to the elders talk. These Sunday visits always included an abundance of traditional foods such as holoptsi (cabbage rolls), perohy, vareneki, borscht, and definitely always lots of homemade bread and fresh butter. Even though the fare was simple, there always seemed plenty to go around, and no one ever left our home hungry. Nor do I ever remember leaving anyone else's home feeling less than completely full.

Genesis 1: 26, 27
"Then God said, 'Let us make human beings in our image, to be like ourselves. They will reign over the fish in the sea, the birds in the sky, the livestock, all the wild animals on the earth, and the small animals that scurry along the ground.'

So God created human beings in his own image.
  In the image of God he created them;
  Male and female he created them."

Chapter 2

Christian Neighbors

One of our closest neighbors and friends was a Ukrainian family. They were very devout Seventh Day Adventists. Two of their children were approximately the same age as my older sister and I. They were also the only girls in our age bracket for miles around, so we naturally became the absolute very best of friends, and remain so to this day. Through time spent with this family, as a child I became aware of ethnic differences as well as differences in life style. For example, every Saturday morning they would drive 10 miles on dirt roads to go into town to attend church, something that our family did not do. They would also take the remainder of that day to rest, even during harvest time - something that was absolutely unheard of in my family. As long as the weather was good, tackling the crops in the fields at harvest time was a job that seemed to have an underlying urgency about it. The men worked from sunup till sundown, and often well into the evening darkness, as late as possible before retiring for the night. Our neighbors, however, always took Saturdays off in order to attend their church and have a day of rest, even though they, too, had crops in the fields, a huge garden, and livestock and poultry to tend to. They also had a book called the Bible, which seemed to be rather important in their household. They talked rather freely about God, something else I was unfamiliar with in our home. Some of the words in the Ukranian language were different from the Russian language that I was familiar with, but the dialect was similar enough that we could easily understand their parents when they spoke to each other as well as to us in Ukrainian. We learned each other's language through visiting each other's families.

Of the many times that I visited their place at mealtime, two things especially stood out in my mind. First, before anyone began reaching for food, even though their plates were in front of them and the food had been placed on the table, every single member of their family put their hands together, bowed their heads down and either looked at their plate or else closed their eyes. Not being familiar with this routine, I did not bow my head nor close my eyes. I just sat there looking around at all of them and wondering what they were doing. Then their father said something out loud about thanking God. I remember looking around, wondering whom he was talking to, since his family didn't appear to be paying any attention to him. They were just all sitting there with their hands together and heads down. I guess I half expected to see God standing in the room somewhere.

He wasn't. I checked.

The father didn't talk long, and rather suddenly everyone said something all at once, something short. Then everyone's heads lifted back up, hands became unclasped, and they started reaching for food on the table. I had no idea how they all knew when to say whatever word it was that they said all at the same time.

Secondly, their borscht had beets in it, of all things. (Doukhobor borscht does not. It is made only with cabbage.) I remember the first time their mother put a bowl of beet borscht in front of me as I sat at their kitchen table. Bad enough it was red, but then she added cream to it, and right there in front of my very eyes, my meal turned a lovely shade of pink. I had never eaten pink borscht before, in all my short life, and my facial expression must have shown it. My friend's mother must have noticed my reaction, and a huge smile crossed her face. Then she gently reassured me that it was Ukrainian style borscht and encouraged me to try it, even though it looked different than the borscht that I was used to seeing and eating. I think I even enjoyed the taste of it, once it had gotten past my eyes.

These differences were very puzzling to me when I was young. I probably asked my parents or else my grandparents about the strange ritual at their mealtime when I got home, but I don't remember what their answer was. If I asked my friends about it, I must not have understood what their reply was, because I just remember it being something I did not understand.

Through this family came my first introduction to church. I don't remember how old I was, but my older sister and I must have pestered my mother and father to let us go to church with the neighbors on Saturday until they gave in and allowed us to go. After all, our friends were going off every Saturday morning, doing something fun, and we wanted to go with them. They had to drive right past our farm to go to their church in town, so it seemed quite practical to us that we should tag along.

I remember going with them inside a huge building which was their church. I was totally awestruck by the glorious sight that awaited me. The windows were the most beautiful I had ever seen. They were not just plain, clear glass, like the windows in our log house and all the houses of our friends and neighbors. Instead they were made of brightly colored pieces of glass which created a picture through which the sun shone. Even the shape of the window was not just a plain square. There were several windows in a row, they were quite narrow and tall, and though the shape was square on the bottom, about three quarters of the way up, the shape changed, and tapered off to a point at the top. The ceiling also seemed very high compared to the log house in which we lived. There were rows and rows of long, planked benches, carved quite fancy on the ends. Many people were sitting on these benches, but some, however, were kneeling on the floor in front of them, with their hands clasped together and their eyes closed, just like I had seen our neighbors doing at mealtime. They were not eating, though. By now, I knew that they were praying. I also knew to be quiet and not bother them or talk to them while they were doing this. In the front of the room I only remember a rather large open area with a high table and other assorted items of "furniture" which were all strange to me.

The entire service was in the Ukrainian language. After a few songs, which were sung loudly and enthusiastically by everyone gathered, there was much talking by one fellow who was dressed very differently. He stood at the front of the room behind a narrow, tall piece of furniture that held a huge book. Our friends explained later that he was the minister, or

20

preacher. I thought that was just a fancy word for a leader of some sort, so that is how I viewed him. During the service, he used many Ukrainian words that I had never heard before and therefore I did not understand. Eventually two ladies stood up and asked all the children to come with them. We got up from our seats and went into a small room at the front of the building, through a door on one side. Here, I remember having a very good time. They told us a children's story, also in Ukrainian, but they used more simple words that I could understand. The story was very different from any stories I had ever heard before, but it was fascinating all the same. Then they gave us crayons and pages of pictures to color, which were pictures from the story we had just heard. We got to take these pictures home with us.

One time that I went to church with our neighbors; there was a change in routine. When the children were called to go to the separate room in the front, I was not allowed to go. My friends went, though. My nose was totally out of joint because I had to stay on the bench with their mom and dad. The preacher talked for a rather long time, it seemed, about something unfamiliar because I could not understand many of the words, again, and then everyone sang more songs I didn't know. Eventually, all the children and the two adults came out from the side room. The children lined up across the front of the church and their 'teachers' stood off to one side. Each child was holding a Bible. The 'teacher' would say one word out loud and all the children would rapidly leaf through their Bibles until one child would shout out that they 'found it'. Then their teacher would say another word, sometimes it was totally unrecognizable to me and other times it was a word I was familiar with, and the children would all quickly leaf thorough their Bibles again until someone again 'found it'. It seemed to me that this little exercise went on for quite some time. I remember thinking that was a very odd thing for them to be doing. Whatever this Bible book was, apparently it must be quite complicated to read if they had to have lessons on how to find things in it, and all the chapter headings were only one word, and some of those words were very weird!

I remember one Saturday morning being dressed up in my 'good clothes' and excitedly waiting for the neighbors to pick me up for church, and they never came. No one had telephones in those days, so there was no way for them to let us know that for whatever reason they were unable to go to town that day. I was hugely disappointed.

I don't know how many times my sister and I actually went to church with them, but not very many, I don't think. As much as we enjoyed this activity, there came a time that our parents must have simply told us that we could not go anymore. I do not remember what reason they gave us. Looking back now, it must have been a very difficult decision for our parents to allow us to even go at all. We were, after all, Doukhobors, with our own culture, beliefs, language, and traditions. Without any sensitivity or understanding of the whole picture of our solid Doukhobor background, we had pestered our parents into letting us try something different just because our friends were doing it.

I used to love Sundays, with the break it brought from everyday routine. Everyone would get his or her assigned chores done as quickly as possible, (at least I did!) in anticipation of companionship that came about by traveling to and visiting at each other's homes. Because there were no telephones, and I am not sure how communications were amongst the adults, but it just seemed to happen, from a kid's point of view, that if no one showed up at our place, we would go out and visit someone. I do remember specific times when our parents would decide on someone to visit, and as we were getting ready to leave, a vehicle would turn into our driveway, bringing with it company to visit us instead. These spontaneous appearances of guests to our farm were always welcomed enthusiastically. Our plans then changed immediately, and a fun time ensued with the present crowd. With eight in our family and most of our visitors also having several children, we were always a crowd. Visits were most often in the afternoons, as everyone had evening chores to tend to. The cows needed milking, poultry had to be fed, all the other animals needed tending to, and basic farm chores had to be done every evening.

Although we almost always visited with our parents, sometimes our grandparents would take us along with them instead, depending on where they were going. One family often had their grandchildren visit them in July and August for several weeks at a time during summer holidays. Their grandchildren were three girls and one boy approximately the same ages as some of us, and we all got along splendidly. I used to look forward to visiting with them from one summer to the next.

On one such warm, sunny Sunday, my grandparents had taken several of us with them to visit these neighbors. Because my grandparents owned a truck, we kids would always ride in the back in the box, while my grandfather drove exceptionally slowly the 2 or 3 miles to their farm. Two of my sisters were in the box with me. We were each standing in our 'own' corner looking out into the clear, starry night, with our backs to each

23

other, when I felt a warm hand gently lay on my shoulder and linger there for a few seconds.

Now this is the part that's crystal clear: I immediately spun around and accusingly demanded, "Who touched me?"

Both of my sisters, each standing a few feet away in their designated corners with their backs to me, just turned around, looked blankly at me, and denied doing so.

In typical sibling fashion and instantly ready for a fight, I accusingly retorted, "Well, somebody touched me!"

Again they both denied doing so. I remember wondering how they managed to get back to their own corners so fast, because anyone with brothers and sisters knows how fast you can whip your head around if there has been unwarranted body contact. I also remember thinking that by the look on their faces, they were telling the truth. Apparently the box of a pick-up truck was not big enough for the three of us that night.

Even though it simply did not make sense, an odd fact remained. Somebody had touched me!

The other strange thing about that incident was that my siblings would have either shouted my name above the wind or else given me an earnest wallop to get my attention. What I felt that evening was definitely not the wind tussling the fabric on the sleeve and back of my shirt or jacket or whatever I was wearing. It was the unmistakable, solid touch of a hand. A warm, gentle hand had been briefly laid on my shoulder.

Jeremiah 1: 5
"Before I formed you in the womb, I knew you. Before you were born, I set you apart...."

Chapter 3

The Spirit World

I grew up listening to older generation family members speak, on a daily basis, and very comfortably, of spirits and souls of the dearly departed. These souls in the spirit world still communicated with loved ones on earth through a variety of ways. They often appeared in dreams, bringing a comforting message or warning of impending danger. Some dreams were more in depth than others, depending on the 'message' that needed to be conveyed at the time, or the emotion that was addressed. Usually these dreams brought about a feeling of comfort. Sometimes the spirits would visibly return to familiar surroundings and 'allow' themselves to be seen again by family members (or very close friends) for just a few seconds in a 'ghostly' state, like transparent smoke just before vanishing away. To the best of my recollection, regardless of how these communications were carried out, these incidents always brought emotional peace or a solution to an issue that somebody here on earth was struggling with.

The men and the women in those days had very specific tasks, and life rolled along in a relatively predictable manner, with everyone routinely doing what was expected of them. Every morning after breakfast, the men would leave their houses to work outside in the fields or in the yard or pasture, on equipment in their garages, with livestock, or one of the very many jobs that needed to be tended to every day. The women had many of their own household chores to tend to. I remember a great number of mornings when my grandmother would walk to our house after she finished her morning chores. She would help my mother as she went about her work, or else relax at the kitchen table and just visit while my mother worked. Besides discussing everyday events, they would more often than not talk about the dreams they had had the night before, or a few days prior. They spoke about who and what their dreams had been about, and sometimes what those dreams might possibly mean in relation to what was happening in their lives at the time. The spirit world, which we could not see, was very much a part of our everyday lives. I was comfortable with the knowledge that there were unseen spirits around us, and firmly believed that they were every bit as real as everything that I could physically see, hear, taste, touch and feel around me.

Good spirits were capable of intervening in our lives in a good way. This was not necessarily always done in a way that was obvious to the eye, but rather something that you could figure out for yourself if you took the time to think about. Most often our emotions were involved. My father and mother would both often tell us to pay attention to what was going on in our lives when we had specific dreams or spiritual encounters. For instance, if one of us was particularly worried or upset about something specific, sometimes that person would have a dream in which there was a subtle message in regards to what was worrying them. Today there is a great deal of literature printed about such positive occurrences, with books and booklets such as 'Guideposts' being one of my favorites.

However, there are good spirits and bad spirits.

Bad spirits, as implied, do destructive things like moving objects or furniture, bring feelings of discontentment, and are also capable of creating bodily harm. I remember the older generation folk saying, in a matter of fact fashion, that the farm where that we were living on had been cursed. The curse had been put onto this farm by someone who had previously lived there.

The family who lived in our house before us witnessed several incidents as a result of this curse. They spoke of strange things that happened for seemingly no reason. The heavy cellar door, on the floor in the living room, would sometimes lift up and down on its own. Their cast iron treadle sewing machine, which stood solidly against a wall, would roll across the floor by itself in the middle of the night. Bizarre things also happened outdoors. Once, when the men were working in one of the fields with horses, suddenly the horses stopped and refused to walk any further into the field. When the men walked ahead of the team of horses to see what was spooking them, there appeared to be a huge, deep ravine in the field that had never been there before. It had simply appeared, virtually out of nowhere. After a period of time, I do not know if it was hours or days, it disappeared again, and the field returned to being as flat and solid as usual. The horses walked there comfortably again.

These incidents were perceived as mere reminders from the spirit world that the land was cursed. Friends and neighbors spoke freely of incidents such as these that also happened on other farms. Although unsettling, they were just a fact of everyday life in the area that we all lived with. As a youngster, I found the stories to be somewhat fascinating in a creepy sort of way while these stories were being told, but I quickly forgot about them as I got distracted by doing something else more interesting, like playing. That included making mud pies that were decorated with sawdust icing and baked on a board in the sun, building forts in the woods in our pasture, making bows and arrows out of willows and old baling twine, or playing cowboys and Indians. At night time, though, I tried not to think about the negative stories from the past, because I would feel very scared if I did.

However, strange things also happened to our family while we were living on that particular farm. Once, my mother awoke in the morning to discover a pile of gray stool on the floor. I remember her saying that it was definitely not human excrement because of the unearthly color and shape, but it was right there on the floor, all the same. She and my father seemed concerned about it, and spoke quietly about how it could not mean anything good.

My brother had a dream when he was a youth that was more specific. He dreamt that he was a younger boy, standing at a very specific spot in our farmyard, looking closely at the maples trees that grew on the east side of our yard near our grandparents house. In the dream, he was contemplating climbing them or maybe building a fort in them. As he stood there scrutinizing the maples trees, he noticed that about midway up or closer to the top were some very odd shaped branches. He realized that camouflaged amongst the branches and leaves, appeared to be hidden some specific letters of the alphabet. Upon closer examination, the branches distinctly spelled out the words "Get Out". He said it was not obvious to the naked eye, and a stranger coming into the yard would not have noticed it. But once you had seen it, and knew where to look, it was very obvious. That dream gave him the creeps. The message to our family from the spirit world was crystal clear.

Sometimes in the summer, us older kids would make beds in a granary beside the house, and sleep out there. One night when we were teenagers, my older sister and I were woken from our sleep in the granary because we heard an unusual noise. It had been raining extremely heavily for several days and our dirt roads were totally impassable. The noise that woke us sounded somewhat like a car engine idling, and partly like a whirring sound. It appeared to be coming from our yard. For some unknown reason that we still cannot explain, we did not feel comfortable opening the door to look outside and see what the noise was. Instead, there in the dark, we cautiously peered out through the one small window. In the extremely heavy rain in the night, we could see a grayish colored car in our yard, and we could hear the enticing sounds of people partying inside, having what sounded to be a very good time. The car's headlights were not on, and we did not recognize whose car it was. We wondered how they managed to drive through the mud to get up the hills to arrive in our farmyard without getting stuck. As appealing as that party appeared to be for us to go out and join, something must not have felt right, because we stayed in the granary and never went outside. What was also unusual was that our dog was not barking, like he always did when company arrived in our yard. My sister has pointed out to me that she remembers thinking how weird it was at the time that our normally protective dog was hiding under the granary we were in, because we could hear him thumping around under our floor. He was at the very back of the granary, as far away as possible from the opening towards the yard. We stayed inside where we felt safe, and eventually went back to sleep.

In the morning when we awoke and went into the house, we asked our mother and father who had been at our place during the night. Seemingly confused, our parents asked us what we meant. When we told them what we had seen and heard, extremely worried looks took over their faces. Neither of them had heard anything unusual. This fact, in itself, was unheard of. My sister and I could not believe that neither of them had heard or seen anything. They were always diligent about being extremely alert to all goings on in and around our yard, and were woken easily at night by much quieter noises than a vehicle idling near the house with loud party goers inside.

Our father's immediate response to us was, "Did you guys go outside?"

When we told him we did not, he appeared to look very relieved. My sister and I did not understand why. We all went out into the yard and retold the nights events to our grandparents. Strangely, they had not heard or seen anything, either. We all looked for tire tracks in the soggy ground in the yard, and there was not a single trace of a vehicle having driven into, being parked in, and then turning around and driving out of our yard again in the night, through the mud and rain.

Several of us also had dreams of a negative nature while we were living there. I remember having one dream in which I was standing outside beside our kitchen window, and sand suddenly started pouring out of the sky over top of me until I was almost buried. In the dream, no sooner did I desperately dig myself out of the pile, when more sand would fall on me and I would be almost buried again. With each attempt to dig myself out, I kept getting reburied. At that point in my dream, I felt a sense of hopelessness that I would never be able to get out of the sand that repeatedly kept burying me. Suddenly, in my dream, a part of me was projected to the middle of the yard from where I could look back and visually see my body being buried under yet more falling sand beside the house. Directly behind the house, peering over the north-west portion of the roof was a huge woman's head. She was holding a gigantic spoon in her massive hand and leisurely continued to effortlessly dump more and more sand over me while I struggled to get free. She was smiling, as if enjoying my terror and helplessness. I woke up feeling a profound sense of despair. I felt like I was a victim of some sort of evil, negative spiritual energy that I would never be free from, because she would never let me escape.

It was not only the spirit world that was capable of upsetting normal daily functions such as the one I mentioned about working the land with horses. In the rural area surrounding us, there were also people in our midst, neighbors known to all, who were said to possess supernatural abilities that they could use for evil. These people in our vicinity were known as black witches. To the best of my memory, in our area at least, these were always women. (Women with supernatural powers who used them for good were called white witches.) In one specific incident near our farm, one farmer began to notice that his cows would not give milk during the morning milking. This was very serious, as everyone in the entire family depended upon the cows yield to provide them with milk, cream, butter, cottage cheese, hard cheese, and buttermilk. Also, any money that could be acquired from the sale of extra cream and butter was needed to buy necessities they could not grow or make themselves.

This family suspected that one neighboring black witch was involved. She supposedly had powers to turn herself into another creature, bird, or animal, at will. The farmer realized that he had to do something. So one night he hid in the barn. In the middle of the night, a strange dog ran in and began milking his cows. The farmer leaped out from his hiding place with a pitchfork or a shovel, hitting the dog several times very hard on the body and face, but intentionally did not kill it. He allowed it to escape into the dark night. The next morning, he made a specific point of going to visit the neighbor whose wife was reputed to have evil powers. When he arrived at the neighbor's farm, the husband told him that his wife was in bed that day and was not feeling at all well. He insisted upon seeing her for himself. She was in bed with broken ribs and a gash on the same area of her face where he had hit the dog with his shovel or pitchfork. Words were spoken between them, and there were no more problems with the cows giving milk again.

I also specifically remember us kids being told not to go into one farm yard because the woman who lived there was a witch, and if we went into her yard, she would turn us into stones. I remember looking, from a distance, at some of the large stones in that yard, and wondering if any of them used

33

to actually be people. We listened to what we were told, though, and never went into that yard without our parents or grandparents present.

Our neighbors from the Ukraine also remember their father telling them about incidents that involved spiritualism back in the old country. He told them of a very powerful spell that he knew of which was used for evil at harvest time. After the fields of grain were ripened in the fall and cut down by hand with a scythe, the wheat was gathered up into stooks. (Stooks are several armloads of hay stood up in a sort of A-frame shape so the wheat kernels are all at the top, to assist drying.) When the heads of wheat were dry, the farmer would go around the field, gathering each stook to store up for the winter. Someone with evil intentions and powers could come into your field, tie several blades of the wheat with a very specific knot, and put a spell on it. When the farmer went to cut down his crop with his scythe, if he happened to even just touch that wheat without noticing the knot, he would die immediately. That is how powerful the spell was. If the person the spell was put upon was a Christian, however, the spell would have no power. This sort of thing, the practicing of witchcraft and spiritualism still goes on in many countries today.

Ephesians 6:10-12

"A final word: Be strong in the Lord and His almighty power. Put on all of God's armor so that you may be able to stand firm against all strategies of the devil. For we are not fighting against flesh and blood enemies, but against evil rulers and authorities of the unseen world, against mighty powers in this dark world, and against evil spirits in the heavenly places."

Chapter 4

Something Very Big Is Out There

Each one of us kids who were raised on that farm had at least one relatively bad 'accident' while we were growing up. None of us died, though. Although our parents did not discuss all of the negative events that took place there in front of us kids, we were told often to learn to be cautious, and be aware of our 'sixth sense' that surely would warn us of wandering into harm's way. We spent many hours playing in the pasture, by the creek, and in the bush by ourselves, far away from the adults. I remember growing up believing that our beloved grandmother had special powers that she used for good, and therefore we were protected, by her, from the not so good spirits that were always around us on that farm that was cursed. Sometimes she would take my little young hands and hold them in her own, then say something in whispers that I did not understand, rather secretive like. If these were prayers, I do not know to whom she prayed. Maybe she prayed to God. I do not know for sure.

She also had some special beans that she used in order to tell fortunes with. She kept these in a small handkerchief which, if I remember correctly, she kept carefully tied up by the four corners in a special knot in order to keep the contents inside. She also collected many roots and herbs in the area, and knew how to use them for healing many common ailments. As a general rule, the Doukhobors in our family were much more comfortable with treating illnesses by natural means than by going to see doctors.

While I was growing up, it was very normal for me to think about spirits, to be comfortable with fortunetellers, and to feel confident that no matter what physical or mental ailment a body had, there was at least one herb or plant in the area that can be used for healing the body's specific ailment. I thought this was a normal way of thinking for everybody.

I also believed that when people passed away, even though their body was buried, their spirit or soul was now free. All spirits, good ones and bad ones alike could now go wherever they wanted to. They had merely passed away from this world. I remember, one day, contemplating the beginning and the end of the life force, the deep down living part of us that is more than the eye can see, the spirits and souls, so to speak. I was wondering how and where I fit into the whole scheme of things. I remember thinking about new babies and aging grandparents, and feeling curious about what was before and after what we were familiar with in the here and now. It seemed rather practical and reasonable to me that surely before a baby is born, their living spirit was out there somewhere, waiting to come to earth into their earthly body. Then, once we have lived out our years here on earth, where did our spirit go after our body physically died? What did it do to pass the time, wherever it was? Would it still be alive somewhere, merely separated from the earthly body that it once used to occupy?

Suddenly I felt as if knowledge, answers, were being poured straight into my brain and thinking process. Immediately, I *knew* that my soul - the very core of my being, the deep down living part of me that was incapable of dying - was eternally connected to an entity of which there was no beginning and no end. Like a ray of light in slow motion from the sun when it creeps above the horizon, this entity spread from the farmyard where I was standing outwards to the neighboring farms, then further to the neighboring towns, across all the prairies and beyond the world that I knew, until it encompassed the entire universe.

Something was in absolute control!

Absolutely nothing went unseen or unheard. Nothing! Everything that I could smell, taste, touch, hear, or see, day or night, everything I could and would ever experience and feel - this same 'something' was in control of it all, including the spirit world.

There was a plan in place! Things did not just happen randomly. There was a reason for everything.

Every single person, animal, plant, tree, bird, fish, rock, hill, creek, lake, ocean, cloud, star, and planet was exactly where it should be, put in place intentionally. Everything had a purpose. I was not in this world by accident. I was one in completeness with an entity that was in control of the entire world.

For some strange reason, I immediately felt very calm and peaceful. As insignificant and unimportant as the kid that I was in the big picture of

37

things, I was now connected to and part of a majestic, living, dynamic force.

I suddenly *knew,* in the most inner core of my very being, that I *was a part of* something absolutely divine.

Luke 10:21,22

"At that same time, Jesus was filled with the joy of the Holy Spirit, and he said, 'O Father, Lord of heaven and earth, thank you for hiding these things from those who think themselves wise and clever, and for revealing them to the childlike. Yes, Father, it pleased you to do it this way. My Father has entrusted everything to me. No one truly knows the Son except the Father, and no one truly knows the Father except the Son and those to whom the Son chooses to reveal him.'"

Chapter 5

The First Voice

One Saturday afternoon of a long weekend when I was in Grade 12, our family drove to the neighboring town of Swan River (as was our weekend routine) to go grocery shopping at the Co-op store at the east end of town. On this particular day I felt strongly compelled, actually physically drawn, to walk several blocks to the west end of town. This was unusual, because we never had any desire to go there, nor to spend any time there. It wasn't because it was a bad part of the town, or anything like that. My siblings and I just did not hang out there. I remember walking along, alone, and thinking how odd it was that I had this overpowering desire that I absolutely *had* to walk to the west part of town, with no rhyme or reason for doing so. It was almost as if I physically could not stop my legs from taking me in that foreign direction.

Just before I got to the railway tracks, I stopped at an intersection where a car had just come to a standstill at the stop sign. I waited for the car on my right to move along so that I could cross the road. One window opened and I heard wolf whistles from some fellows inside the car.

Suddenly, I heard the words, *"You're going to marry that man"* clearly 'spoken' to me in my head.

The car drove away, and I remember standing there and thinking that this was a very strange and mysterious thing that had just happened to me. Where did that voice come from? *Who* said that? What kind of message was that, anyway? I was only seventeen years old and in grade twelve. Marriage was not something I was concerned about yet. I did not recognize the car as a local one, nor did I recognize anyone inside as familiar faces.

As soon as the car drove away, my obsession to keep walking in that direction also disappeared. I turned around, walked back to the part of town where I usually hung out, and resumed what was a normal day in every other way. I remember thinking that the occurrence was very odd, in a supernatural sort of way. Also, the voice was most certainly one which I did not recognize. Although my life was full and busy, I felt extremely puzzled about what had happened. The incident struck me as so bizarre that I do not remember telling anyone about it, except maybe my sisters.

Nothing about that experience on the west end of town made sense. I had to finish high school before venturing out into the world on my own. How and where would I ever find this guy again? I had never even gotten a clear look at any one of the faces. And who spoke to me, about something so strange? And where did that clear voice come from?

This was just plain weird!

High school was a busy time in my life, so I do not remember dwelling on it very much, probably because I could not make sense of it. I never forgot the incident, though.

When I finished Grade 12, I moved out of home and got a job about two and a half hours away in the northern town of The Pas. At last, I was independent. Finally! I was out on my own! This was a very exciting time in my life. I got hired almost immediately as a telephone operator, and made friends very easily with several girls my age who were also recent high school graduates. We all had full time jobs for the first time in our lives.

Two of my roommates at this time were also young ladies who grew up on small farms, about one hour and fifteen minutes away from where I grew up, so we had a lot in common. We were country bumpkins on an adventure at an extremely jubilant point in our lives. The only one thing we really *had* to do was appear at the telephone office and work our full time shifts. For this simple task, we were regularly rewarded with what seemed like a very generous pay cheque to spend, however we chose to. Once a month we had rent to pay, and when the fridge got empty, we had to buy groceries to feed ourselves. Even this task was a pleasure. We could buy whatever we wanted to eat! There was no school, no homework or assignments, no parents finding something for us to do, no outside yard work, no vegetable garden to plant or weed, no family obligations of any sort whatsoever. Our time off was ours to enjoy fully! We enjoyed eating out, going to shows, and shopping for clothes. At that time there was a strict dress code in place for all telephone operators, so we really did need a decent work wardrobe. Whenever we had days off back to back, we

41

could easily afford a bus ticket home for a couple of days if we were homesick.

My friends and roommates, of course, shared the same interests as me. In this case, our idea of a good time almost always involved parties, going to bars, and drinking, most often to excess. My 'mornings after' often arrived with a pounding headache, an upset stomach, and unpleasant memories of reckless behavior and stupid words spoken while under the influence of alcohol. Even though I always felt remorseful about my actions for a few days, by the next weekend I would party hearty with my friends, and act stupid all over again. It was a cycle of so called 'fun', and no one talked about any feelings of remorse, shame or regret because not one of us was going to be the first one to admit that this destructive lifestyle was actually harmful to our wellbeing.

I did miss my family, though. When I first left home, our house did not have a telephone. When my parents did get one, long distance charges were relatively expensive, so phone calls home were few and far between, and were always kept to a minimum time frame. I would write letters home, though, to both my parents and individual siblings in English. They would write back to me also, and a new form of communication began with my family. Oh, the comfort I used to receive from the loving letters from my family. Even though I could fluently speak Russian, and could recite the Russian alphabet that my grandmother had taught me, I did not know how to read or write the language, so therefore I could not communicate with my grandparents. They, on the other hand, were totally fluent speaking, reading, and writing in Russian. They could speak a little

English, but could not read or write it, nor did they have a telephone. Not being able to communicate with them saddened me greatly.

It did not take long for a solution to arrive in the mail one day. I eagerly ripped open an envelope from home, addressed to me in my mother's handwriting. There, staring back at me, was a letter in an older person's handwriting (it was a bit shaky), written entirely in Russian! My darling grandmother had very lovingly written me a letter in the only way she knew how. There, at the top of the page, she also wrote out the entire Russian alphabet. Above each letter of the alphabet, in my mother's handwriting, was written in English the sound that that letter made. Our communication problem was solved! All I had to do was find the first letter of the first word somewhere in the alphabet at the top, sound it out, figure out and find the next letter, sound it out, find the third letter, sound it out, so on and so forth, until one word was "read", then go on to the next word. Thus began my learning to read and write in Russian. To write a letter back to her, the process was merely done in reverse. I would sound out what I wanted to say, and find each letter of every word, one by one, in that alphabet at the top of the original letter, write it down, and move on to the next sound in the word. Simple!! Extremely time consuming, but very simple! Amazingly enough, it did not take very long before I could recognize some of the more commonly used words to read. There even came a time that I did not need to refer to that original letter with the Russian alphabet at the top in order to read mail from my grandmother and grandfather, or to write back to them. I always kept that letter, and have it to this day. Actually I kept all the letters written to me by my grandparents. Many years later, once when my mother was visiting us, I pulled out this precious bundle of mail and she read them all out loud. It was fantastic. It was just like having a visit with them.

My life at this point was as much of a whirlwind as I wanted to make it. My friends and I would sometimes go to tea cup readers and fortune tellers on a whim, half paying attention to what they predicted or foretold, and half not. We would read our horoscopes, trying to find similarities between what was written there and what actually happened in our lives, or more likely, what we made happen after reading the horoscopes. We would read pamphlets that told you what your personality was like based on your birthday, and try to figure out how close they came. We would show an interest astrology predictions based on some sort of personal information and believe to a tiny degree that this might actually come to be. In a sense, I suppose we were figuring out who we were. One of my roommates had a Ouija board that we played with sometimes, but on one occasion, I recall feeling positive that I saw the pointer thing move by itself. That totally creeped me out, and I did not play with the Ouija board after that.

Days off continued to be spent enjoying the drinking and partying scene that became our lifestyle. We stayed in the yo-yo cycle of drinking to excess, feeling bad about what we had said and done when we sobered up, and then doing it again the next weekend anyway. After all, this was what everybody around us was doing, so that made it 'acceptable' and okay to keep doing. Sometimes I would feel angry for days at a time, and not really be able to pinpoint why. On those days I would wear my appropriate 'Mad Russian' sweatshirt. It had a picture on the front of it of a cartoon styled Russian man with a furious expression on his face.

Romans 7:15-17, 22, 23

"I don't really understand myself, for I want to do what is right, but I don't do it. Instead, I do what I hate. But if I know that what I am doing is wrong, this shows that I agree that the law is good. So I am not the one doing wrong: it is sin living in me that does it. ...I love God's law with all my heart. But there is another power within me that is at war with my mind. This power makes me a slave to the sin that is still within me."

It was during this time in my life that I met the tall, dark, and handsome man from Nova Scotia who would become my husband. He was definitely the one for me! Some of my girlfriends and I have recently talked about this. Several of us just instinctively *knew* when we met the young men who would become our husbands, that they were 'the one' for us.

As we dated and I got to know him better, there came a time when I gathered up the courage to question him about the possibility of him being in the town of Swan River at that particular intersection on the exact Saturday of the long weekend prior when I had heard the strange voice telling me that I was going to marry the man in the car. After some deliberate focus on his activities of the past year, prompted by my specific questions, he tied incidents together of what was happening in his life at the time, and he confirmed that he and a carload of his buddies had indeed passed through Swan River on the exact Saturday of that particular long

45

weekend, while they were traveling from The Pas to Winnipeg. At that time, there was only one main highway through town from the north. Calculating the time of day when they would have been at that exact intersection on the main highway coincided closely with the time of day that I felt compelled to walk there, and heard a voice.

I also remember him asking me why I was quizzing him about his whereabouts on a long weekend in which I never even knew him. I suppose it *was* a rather strange question to ask a relatively new boyfriend. I believe my answer to that was to downplay my interest, once I got my information, and just say that I was curious, that's all. I tried to act like it was no big deal. Besides, I doubted that he would believe me if I told him that I heard a voice telling me we would marry. Even if he did believe me and entertain the idea that I was telling the truth about hearing a voice, he would surely head for the hills as fast as his legs could carry him, to get away from this nutty female who claimed to hear voices. I thought it much better to keep this information to myself! That is, at least, until I got to know him a bit better. To this day, he doesn't believe in spiritual "stuff", but I know I was led there for a reason, it was God who spoke to me then, and that it was Him in that car. His answer to me confirmed it.

We dated for a while, both drinking heavily and partying whenever we were not working. To this day, I do not know anyone whose personality is enhanced by alcohol consumption, but it is a lifestyle that is effortless to fall in to, and easily accepted, especially by many young adults. We dated, lived together, and got married. We lived in several towns in northern Manitoba before embarking on an adventure to the Yukon. Our friends had recently moved there and invited us to come up, telling us that we would love it there. Our friend could get my husband a job at the mine in Faro. We decided it would be a great adventure to go north where neither of us had ever been before, at least for the summer months when it was relatively warm in northern Canada. Jobs were readily available everywhere, in those days, so we figured that we could find jobs again when we came back to the prairies.

We stopped in at my parent's home to say goodbye to everyone. I felt a wee bit apprehensive about going so far away from my family, but I was also young and excited to be off on an adventure with my new husband. When I said goodbye to my beloved grandmother and grandfather, my grandmother became very sad and got tears in her eyes. In Russian, she told me that she would not see me again. I reassured her that she would, because we were not planning on being up north for long.

She just looked at me with tears in her eyes and said in Russian, "No, dear one, I will not see you again."

We hugged and she kissed me the Russian way – first one cheek, then the other cheek, then on the forehead. We hugged some more and both cried. This goodbye was a very difficult one for me.

I was very saddened by her words, because she had never spoken like that before, and besides, she had been there my whole life. Maybe in my young, naive way, I just never thought about death. I had not lost anyone close to me yet. On the drive up to the Yukon, I convinced myself that she just did not like to see us go so far away, and that is why she felt she would

47

never see us again. Surely she was just feeling that way because she was getting old and we were going far away for the first time.

In the wisdom of the elders, however, she was right. She never did see me again. We had left for the Yukon in the spring, and she passed away the following winter on Christmas day. I was seven months pregnant when we drove home for the funeral, and this confirmed what I had heard the elders speak of for years: when one generation ends, a new life often begins. There seems to be a sort of predestined plan in place for continuation of life in families.

We ended up staying in the Yukon for six years. While there, we were blessed with two beautiful baby girls and became a family. Life stayed busy, but in a very different way. Gone were the carefree days of looking after only ourselves. Instead, we had babies to tend to, and our days became occupied with the joys and responsibilities of raising wee ones. I left the workforce to become a stay at home mom while my husband worked at the mine.

Several years later, my grandfather also passed away. I was devastated by his death, because I had always felt very close to him, since he and my grandmother lived in the same farmyard as us all of my growing up years. His funeral marked the end of an era in my life. All I had left were pictures and memories of these two wonderful people who had been such an important part of my life. This saddened me greatly, and I missed living close by to my family and being able to freely speak of my grandparents with people who had also known them well. My husband had known them very briefly, and was as supportive as possible to my sadness. He and my grandfather had gotten along beautifully in their own special way. My grandfather could speak very little English, and my husband could speak no Russian. Yet they seemed to enjoy each other's company in a simple, heartwarming way, especially when they watched wrestling matches together on TV.

One day while my husband and I were going for a drive, I was feeling particularly isolated by distance from my core family, and extremely sad about the loss of my grandparents. Exactly then, we drove past two crows sitting on a telephone wire near the road. I noticed that they were just sitting there, looking intently at our vehicle as it went by. It was immediately impressed upon me that these two crows were not what they seemed. These were the spirits of my grandfather and my grandmother. I got the feeling that they were here to let me know that regardless of the distance between me and all my family at home, the spirits of my grandparents would always be near me. I did not have to feel like I was isolated from them at all. The spirit world that I was so familiar with on the prairies was capable of traveling to be here with me in our mountain home, two thousand miles away. I was very comforted by the knowledge that I was not really 'separated' from my spiritual roots by the vast distance that separated us physically. I experienced a certain amount of peace in regards to our geographical location after that, at least for a while.

Psalm 34:18
"The Lord is close to the brokenhearted;
He rescues those whose spirits are crushed."

49

Chapter 6

Major Changes

Over the next few years, we moved several times. My husband's job took us to live in the mining towns of Fernie, Kitsault, and Logan Lake, -all in different parts of British Columbia. As a young family, we were very busy. Our children were involved in many activities both in school and out. We belonged to different organizations wherever we happened to be living. We always seemed to own several pets at a time, everything from goldfish, dogs, cats, a dwarf rabbit and hamsters. We enjoyed boating, camping, and fishing. We also delighted in sitting around fires at night cooking hot dogs and marshmallows, both with our friends and also extra kids who happened to come along with us.

When I was 34 years old, my father got diagnosed with cancer. He was not doing well, so we decided that I should go back home to Manitoba to spend some time with him and my mother. While I was there, my father was transferred to a hospital in Winnipeg. My mother and I flew down with him and were fortunate enough to be able to stay at the home of very dear friends of our family. They had been our next door neighbors and excellent friends of the family for many years before moving to the city.

They graciously opened their home to my mother and all of my siblings who happened to come to visit our father in the hospital for the duration of his stay. They are two of the most kind and caring people that I have ever had the pleasure of knowing.

My mother and I spent all our time at the hospital with my father, and only went to our friend's house to sleep at night. In time, I had to go back home to my husband and daughters, regardless of how bad the situation was with my father. After I bought a bus ticket from Winnipeg to Kamloops so that I could return home, I went to the hospital to see my father for the very last time. I had a very sickening feeling that I would never see him again, and this fact left me feeling totally devastated. We managed to say our goodbyes, and I tried not to be too upset in front of him. He had enough on his plate already, dealing with cancer, without me bawling like a baby in front of him. I did not even know what to say to him. What do you say to the father who has raised you when you know you will never see him again? He just sat on that hospital bed in his white gown, looking so small. Although I managed to control my emotions at least somewhat while we were with him, as soon as we left his hospital room, I cried all the way back to our friend's house. I did not get much sleep that night, but just kept waking up and crying. Morning came as it always does, and I had to physically drag myself up and out of bed. I tried not to be too upset in front of my mother, but I'm sure that she could see right through me. We went to the bus depot, I said goodbye to my mother, and I boarded the bus.

I was beside myself with torment. In minutes, I would be driving away and knew I would never see my loving father again. As far as my mother,

I felt absolutely heartbroken for her. I was leaving her standing there all alone, just looking so sad and lost in the city, watching the bus pull away. This was definitely not going to be an easy trip, not one little bit. My mood changed from devastating sadness to fury. In a move out of character for me, I intentionally sat in an aisle seat on the bus, and shot the most vicious glare I could muster up at anyone who looked like they may be even slightly entertaining the idea of sitting beside me in the window seat. It was easy to do because I meant it. It worked! Everyone boarding the bus avoided me, and the empty window seat beside me remained vacant. I was not feeling friendly in the least, and I definitely did not want anyone to sit beside me and put me in a situation where I would have to make small talk. That would only happen 'over my dead body' on this trip. The rest of the passengers could like it or lump it, as I did not care one little bit. They could all stay as crowded as they were. I was not going to share the empty seat beside me with anyone. Period!

When the bus began to pull away from the depot, my feelings of fury and devastation escalated rapidly. I felt guilty because I was leaving my father to die of cancer, and there was not a single, solitary thing I could do about it. I was leaving my mother behind to deal with this massive burden without my help. As much as I longed to remain in Winnipeg and support my mother and spend precious time with my very sick father, I needed to be at home with my husband and my daughters. I was terribly torn in two directions.

I was emotionally overwhelmed in this dilemma, and there was nothing I could do but cry. I was physically trapped in a cramped Greyhound bus seat all while becoming emotionally unglued. I sobbed uncontrollably for miles while the bus roared down the highway. There was a young man from Newfoundland sitting across the aisle from me. At one point in a lull of my tears, he asked me in a very nice way what was wrong. When I tried to tell him, I started crying all over again. He didn't talk to me anymore. I worked myself up into a state of complete and utter panic. I distinctly remember thinking that there was absolutely no way in the world that I could travel in this state of mind for the next thirty hours or so, however long the bus ride was. Then I decided that this was it – this must be what it feels like to be totally and entirely out of control and on the edge of insane. How on earth was I ever going to manage this long bus ride feeling like this? I could not. No way. I was definitely going to lose my mind. Then what was the bus driver going to do with me, in the middle of nowhere?

Right about then, the bus pulled to a stop at a depot in yet another sleepy little town on the prairies on the Trans-Canada highway. A few people were standing around outside together, waiting to board. From where I was sitting, one man appeared to look strangely familiar. I couldn't believe my eyes. This guy looked exactly like my father! Even in my miserable emotional state, my curiosity was peaked. As the passengers boarded the bus one by one and started walking down the aisle, sure enough, there he was, coming straight towards me. The closer he came, the more I realized that he really *did look* exactly like my father. When he got right in front of me, he stopped walking, glanced at the empty window seat beside me, and then looked into my eyes with an expression that wordlessly asks for permission to join a stranger in their space. I moved my legs to one side so that he could get past me in order to sit in the window seat that I had been hogging the whole trip so far. He did not say anything. He just smiled politely at me, squeezed past my knees, and sat down. All of a sudden, crying was the furthest thing from my mind.

This was something totally new to deal with. At this point, I very seriously questioned my sanity completely, because my eyes were now seeing my father sitting right beside me! That was absolutely impossible, of course. But, at the same time, this guy *was* my father. Everybody has their own scent, and this man had my father's. I intentionally took in a very deep breath through my nose, as nonchalantly and quietly as possible. Yes, it was definitely him. I did not want to make him uncomfortably by staring at him, so I tried not to. I just watched him as best as I could in my peripheral vision,

How could he be real? Obviously he could not, but here he was, sitting right next to me and I had to deal with that. I decided that I needed to investigate this phenomena a bit more. Casually, I moved my hand over onto the arm rest between us and stuck my finger out. I could feel the fabric on his jacket with the tip of my finger. Was there a body under there making it hold its shape? He was definitely real, and I could see his chest rise and fall ever so slightly with every breath. When, in my peripheral vision, I saw him looking out the window, I turned and had a really good look at him. Even the whiskers on his cheek and neck were my father's. Every hair was in just the right place and exactly the right color. How fascinating! This was definitely my father sitting here beside me as the Greyhound bus roared west downs the Trans-Canada highway.

For reasons I cannot explain, as weird as this situation was, in time I felt strangely comforted by the presence of my father in the seat next to me.

As the miles rolled on by, I was able to calm down a bit, and eventually to even relax. I never spoke to him, though. What can you possibly say to an apparition? As the bus rumbled down the highway, he eventually leaned his head against the window and dozed off. I felt sorry that I did not have a pillow to offer to him, because the glass window was so cold and hard and must have been uncomfortable, although he appeared to be resting just fine. Mile after mile rolled by, prairie town after prairie town fell away behind us, and eventually, I, too, fell into an exhausted sleep, calmed by the presence of my father beside me. In my deep state of slumber, I was only slightly aware of the bus stopping and starting many times as passengers got on and off at different towns along the road. At one point, when the bus stopped yet again to let passengers disembark or load up, I was vaguely aware of someone brushing by me. The next time I woke up, the seat next to me was empty, and he was gone. I took full advantage of the extra room and stretched out across both seats, falling into a deep sleep.

When I awoke, I felt much better. I was relaxed, calm, and thinking rationally again. I was very relieved to discover that my mind was intact after all. I thought long and hard about the phenomena on the bus. Obviously, my father was still in his bed at the hospital back in Winnipeg. There was no way he popped out for a joy ride on the bus. But the man on the bus in the seat next to me was real, also. I had felt his jacket, breathed in the familiar scent, and seen the whiskers on his face. None of that made the least bit of sense. The only thing that had changed was that I felt better now. I was calm and at peace. I had known all along that I needed to go home to be with my husband and my daughters in Logan Lake, B.C., but I was now okay with it.

The rest of the trip was uneventful. At some point during the trip, the Newfie in the seat across from me and I had a short, normal conversation about nothing in particular that travelling strangers have. I thought I owed him at least that much. I wanted to ask him if he saw the man sitting beside me for a while, but thought better of it. If he said no, he had not seen anyone at all sitting beside since we left Winnipeg, I would not know what to do with that information.

My father passed away shortly thereafter. It had only been approximately three months since he was originally admitted into the hospital for pain in his back. The funeral service was a very surreal activity. I was there and it was happening, but I felt totally numb. So many people came to pay their respects at his service, they had to stand outside of the Doukhobor Prayer Home, on the steps and in the yard. Afterwards, the funeral procession travelled to the cemetery and we stood through a short ceremony there. The casket containing my father's body was lowered into the ground, and then came that agonizing, final moment when everything was finished.

There is absolutely nothing left to do for anyone who is gathered there to mourn except to turn around and walk away, leaving your loved one behind in the cold ground in their final resting place. How could we just leave him there all alone and cold, and just walk away? I remember feeling so extremely heartbroken that there was no way to even express myself. I had reached a new state of dark, deep numbness and grief. I felt dead inside.

Suddenly, for the first time that afternoon, the clouds parted and the sun came out from behind them. An almost unrealistic feeling of peace and warmth swept over me while I was standing at the cemetery on that hilltop, mentally wrestling with having to leave my father behind in this permanent, remote place. Basking in the unexpected warmth, I felt something akin to an emotional reassurance that in the long run, everything was going to be all right.

I have spoken to my family about this unnatural feeling of warmth and peace that came over us at that time, and we all felt it. It was like a little wave of comfort that swept over us like a tender, loving caress.

After we returned home to B.C., I went through a period of time when I felt positively miserable. No one in Logan Lake had known my parents, with exception of a couple of our friends who had met them briefly. I found it hard to heal since I never heard his name spoken, unless my husband and children and I talked about him ourselves.

Not only that, I was also very worried about my youngest siblings. My youngest sister was only eighteen years old, and the province of Manitoba considered her an orphan. That broke my heart. My only brothers were merely twenty-three and twenty-five years old. They were much too young to be left without a father figure in their lives. Myself, my older sister, and my younger sister (three years younger than I) would have to be all right somehow, because we were the oldest. My heart went out to the youngest ones.

One evening I went to bed feeling particularly sad and helpless about this new situation in the family. There was nothing I could do to comfort my youngest siblings, with living so far away from everyone, and it really bothered me. I had a very restless night. The next morning, when I awoke and came out of the bedroom, I noticed that the kitchen door was ajar. I remember looking at it and feeling puzzled, because one thing my husband was very diligent about was locking the doors at night. I was the first one up that morning and everyone else was still sleeping, so no one had been in or out yet. Suddenly, I experienced a quiet, comforting feeling, along with the knowledge that this was a sign from my father. He had visited us from the spirit world during the night or early morning, and had left the door open a little so we would know that he had been here. I immediately experienced a reassuring feeling that my youngest sister and my brothers were going to be fine, and I did not have to worry about them. I had a strong sense that from his new home in the spirit world, he was looking out for them somehow. I felt comforted, and to some degree, my worry lessened. As long as my father was in the spirit world watching over us, we would all be all right. Life was going to be different now, that was all.

Ephesians 2: 12

"In those days, you were living apart from Christ. ... You lived in this world without God and without hope."

Chapter 7

A Voice I Know

As our daughters grew up in B.C., we visited family in Manitoba and Nova Scotia whenever time and money would allow. We felt that it was important for them to know their extended family, but we lived so far away. While they were young, we made family trips together. As they got older, they were able to spend summer holidays in Manitoba on their own, staying with their grandmother, and seeing all their cousins and aunties and uncles, since all the family members were within a one hundred mile radius of each other at the time. We usually drove them out there, or else my mother would come out to our place for a visit, then they would go back to the prairies with her. In one particular year, we were not planning a trip back, nor was my mother planning on coming out for a visit. When I checked the bus schedules, if they got on at Kamloops, they would have to change buses in Edmonton, as well as wait at the bus depot for several hours alone between buses. We felt that they were still too young to change buses safely in a major city alone, and that it would be safer if I drove them as far as Edmonton to put them on a Greyhound bus there. That way, they would stay on the same bus for the entire trip, and they also would not have to spend time alone in a major city waiting to change buses.

When the time came to leave, my husband was working so my friend agreed to come on the drive with me. We left after work with the girls, and drove part way to Blue River, where we spent the night at a hotel. Their bus left from Edmonton around noon the next day. We went to sleep, and during the night, towards early morning, I experienced what started out as a dream. In my dream, I was in a house somewhere when the phone began to ring. When I answered it, my grandfather Zebrow's voice was on the other end of the phone (he had passed away years before.)

He spoke only eight words; *"Go home on the bus with the girls."*

I was shocked.

Where did *that* come from? But oh, was it ever wonderful to hear his voice again. I had not heard it for so long. Why was my grandfather telling me that, though? Not only that, why on earth was this message given to me now instead of while we were still at home in Logan Lake? We were already half way to Edmonton. Arrangements were already in place for my mother to pick up the girls at a specific bus depot in Saskatchewan, and then take them to her home in Manitoba. She lives only six miles from the provincial boundary. What could possibly be wrong with putting them on the bus as we planned?

60

Very quickly, logic kicked in. Of course, buses are safe. Besides, my friend is traveling with me. What am I supposed to tell her? We're in my car. She'll think I'm positively loony if I change all the plans after our trip has already begun, and just because I heard a voice in a dream? Good grief! After all, only crazy people hear voices. I most certainly could not tell her what had just happened. Was my dear, loving grandfather warning me of impending danger? It was so nice to hear his voice again, even under these circumstances. It would have been nice if he had elaborated some more, and added an explanation in his very short message to me. I lay awake for the rest of the early morning, literally tormented by this horrible dilemma.

In my traditional Doukhobor beliefs and way of thinking, I knew that the living spirits of my deceased ancestors, grandparents included, were very much alive somewhere, nearby, and I always felt that they were somehow keeping a protective watch over me and all of my family. So it's not that I was freaked out about hearing my grandfather's voice. That part gave me the warm fuzzies. The absolutely upsetting part to me was the message itself.

I fretted extensively about how I could possibly explain to my friend and my daughters my reasoning for changing plans. The truth would have to include me telling them about hearing the voice of my grandfather. Normal people just don't *do* that. I decided not to tell any of them about the strange incident, and to continue the trip as planned.

What a horrible mistake that was!

On the remainder of the drive from Blue River to Edmonton, I relentlessly drilled as much safety advice into my children as possible:

"Be sure to sit in the front near the bus driver, and on the side where he can see you."

"Be sure to sit together."

"Tell the bus driver if anything at all seems wrong."

"Be sure to sit together."

"Do not get off the bus at all, anywhere along the road." (I had packed them a lunch and drinks) "Be sure to sit together."

"Do not talk to anyone else."

"Absolutely do not take anything from anyone to eat or drink, not as much as a piece of gum."

"Above all, phone me the minute you get to Yorkton, so that I know you got there safely.'

"Be sure to sit together."

When I wasn't giving them safety tips out loud, I was inwardly pleading with my grandfather to go on that bus ride with them and protect them from whatever unseen negative thing that prompted this whole commotion to begin with.

I was absolutely *sick* when the bus pulled away with my daughters on it. I know that I was very poor company on the return trip home. Ninety-nine percent of my thoughts were elsewhere, as one percent was needed to drive.

Silently, I repeated safety phrases to myself the whole trip back, but I don't know to whom I said these. Maybe to my grandfather, since it was his voice that delivered the message. I think it was more of a panic thing, a feeling that if I said something enough times, surely somewhere, somehow, some kind of power out there in the universe would hear me and help.

"Keep my girls safe and delivered into my mother's care" was said over and over again in my head.

I may have even asked angels to keep watch over them. My grandmother had two pictures of angels watching over children in her house that I used to love to look at. Angels seem to be acceptable in today's society. Angels were good beings, spirits, and maybe they would hear my pleas and step in to help.

Regardless, I felt positively sick to my stomach. I finally told my friend about the dream as we were driving home, because it was consuming me totally. I could not concentrate on having a normal conversation with her as long as this was eating away at my mind. She made no real comment back to me, neither positive or nor negative. She probably thought that she was trapped in the car with a nutcase.

My girls did arrive safely. I grilled them over the phone about the trip, and everything seemed uneventful. Nothing was out of the ordinary for them. Later, I thought that maybe I was meant to be in Manitoba for some reason, but nothing ever materialized in that respect either.

I am not sure why I got that message from my grandfather at this time. Maybe angels did hear a desperate mother's pleas and avert some kind of wrongdoing or disaster that my grandfather's words warned of. I guess I will never know, or maybe I will know when I stand before Jesus after leaving this earthly life.

Psalm 91: 11, 12
"For he will order his angels
To protect you wherever you go
They will hold you up with their hands
So you won't even hurt your foot on a stone."

Chapter 8

The Vision

As mentioned earlier, I grew up in a very tight knit Doukhobor farming community, speaking the Russian language, and was fully immersed in timeless traditions which had been carried on from generation to generation. My spiritual beliefs also came from these same ancestors, and formed the way of thinking which resulted in decisions I made in my life as an adult. My husband, on the other hand, was raised in military bases in Eastern Canada, as his father was in the navy. His life involved moving often, from base to base, as a child and youth. They were used to living for short periods of time near new neighbors from many different walks of life. We had to learn to work out many major differences in our backgrounds when we set up a home together.

As exciting as it was traveling around and living in different parts of the country with my husband and children, there was always a part of me that longed to live close to my family. I felt a very strong desire, almost a need, for them to grow up surrounded by family, as I had done. I wanted them to be well grounded in their roots, like I had grown up. I also felt like I was missing out on time with my mother, my one grandmother who was still alive, my brothers and sisters and their spouses, my nieces and nephews, aunts and uncles, and cousins. On long weekends and holidays, my family on the prairies always got together for visits, and I would usually phone home and have a turn talking to everyone and anyone who happened to be in my mother's house at the time. Very often after these phone calls I would feel very homesick.

I began to seriously question the path that my life was going on. I was beginning to wonder how everyone in my core family seemed able to remain in close proximity except me. My husband had tried to get work nearer to home, but those jobs never materialized. We just seemed destined to live far away, and I was not enjoying it any more. Something was missing in my life. It had to be my mother and all the rest of my core family. What else could it possibly be? I had known nothing else in my life that I could be missing so desperately, so it had to be them.

Ecclesiastes 3:11

"Yet God has made everything beautiful for its own time. He has planted eternity in the human heart, but even so, people cannot see the whole scope of God's work from beginning to end."

Since my father passed away, I felt even more despondent with my geographical location. While we had been at home for the funeral, many friends and neighbors spoke fondly of him and shared many stories of interactions with him. I found it very comforting to be amongst lifelong friends and neighbors with whom my father had interacted on a daily basis.

Upon coming back to our home in Logan Lake, I felt extremely separated from my roots at this devastating time in my life. No one here had really known him, so no one spoke of him. I did have several very close girlfriends who were very supportive of what I was going through, and we did spend a lot of time talking, as women often do. I had to force myself to stay somewhat upbeat to keep life normal for my children's sake.

I have always loved going for long walks, and my preference is to be out in the bush, the wilds, totally surrounded by nature, where my dog can run free, and I can enjoy the wonders of the forest and meadows around me. The only times I walked through town was if there had been cougar sightings nearby, after dark so that I was in the streetlights, or else after a hard rain when the dirt roads in the bush were too muddy to make walking enjoyable.

During this very sad time in my life, I remember going for my walks around town and sometimes being in the area of the community church, as it was spring, and the dirt roads were muddy. On these occasions, I would often experience a strong desire to go inside, although I did not really understanding why.

In fact, it was extremely puzzling that I was even drawn to the church at all. While I was growing up, any talk associated with churches and preachers almost always had a swear word preceding it. Catholics, especially, were spoken of with contempt, and I always felt it was safest and best to simply avoid all religions altogether. I should just stick with what I knew to be good and true, the Doukhobor way in which I was so lovingly raised.

67

Some elderly individuals in our community who had survived the persecution in Russia had horrific scars on their bodies, and told unimaginable, nightmarish stories of being tortured. But they were the lucky ones. They were alive. When my grandparents and their friends, (the elders of the community) spoke of these incidents, it was their grandparents, great-grandparents, mothers, fathers, sisters, brothers, good friends and neighbors that they were emotionally speaking of. My mother remembers seeing her grandfather's back, which was very deeply scarred with crisscross lines from whippings that had torn away chunks of flesh. The wounds from persecution by the church and the Czarist State in the 'old country' were intensely personal.

And yet, knowing and remembering all my history, here I was, feeling inexplicably drawn to this adorable little community church on the hilltop at Logan Lake, with an awesome view of Mamet Lake in the distance. Everything about my attraction to this church was just plain wrong, on so many levels. I felt terribly guilty that I was even entertaining thoughts of going into a church.

As appealing as that little church seemed to be, I could not bring myself to go inside. Nobody just walks in off the street! Either you go to church or you don't, for all of your life. That was my firm belief. Considering our background, nobody in my immediate family had ever gone to a church of any kind; therefore I clearly did not belong there. I felt it was easier for my brothers and sisters to stay true to our roots, keeping to the same line of thinking and beliefs, because they were all still relatively close together geographically. They saw each other often enough to be supportive whenever trials came along. Also, there were still a lot of Doukhobors in that area, so they had the comfort of belonging to the majority of the population. I, on the other hand, felt very alone.

My mother was an extremely realistic and well-grounded lady, and will always be my role model. Her philosophy was to live decently, work hard, and always be good to those around you. The way in which she lived her life reflected this beautifully, and I have always looked up to her shining example of how to respectfully treat all people in all situations. It was simple. Live right and you will be happy. She was happy with her life. My husband was happy with his life. My friends were all happy with their lives. I found it quite frustrating that I could not find the same measure of happiness and peace in my own life that everyone close to me seemed to be able to acquire so seemingly effortlessly.

No amount of gardening, sewing, walking, cooking traditional foods, reading, visiting with friends, or enjoying my husband and children made me feel completely content. Something was missing in my life. I entertained the idea of walking into the friendly looking little church some more. If I did go in, what would I say if someone asked me something, like 'why was I there?' I couldn't just blurt out to these people that felt like I had a big, empty hole in my heart, - a massive void that nothing seemed to be able to fill, since my father had passed away. Many of the "church goers" were acquaintances I knew from around town. They were all nice enough people, but church was their thing, - it wasn't mine. I didn't mind visiting with them uptown and talking about topics we had in common, but I certainly would not be able to start going to church and 'becoming one of them'. Not only that, I was quite certain that my husband would not be pleased if I took up going to church, as my family came first. Now, when I look back to this point in my life, I realize that my fierce dedication to my roots and my desire to not 'rock the boat' in my family was what I based my decisions on.

The void in my life had to be filled with something.

I began going to a meditation group. Going to this meditation group seemed more acceptable to me somehow. In this group, there was much talk about the spirit world, which I was very comfortable discussing. Although I was not familiar with meditation itself, I was extremely comfortable with and even somewhat knowledgeable on the topic of spirits. Maybe that was because it was not a formal institution like a church. Several of us just met casually at one person's home once a week. My friend and I jokingly called these our 'spook meetings'.

Proverbs 14:12
"There is a path before each person that seems right, but in the end it leads to death."

Here we were kept busy learning all kinds of new, spiritual ways to look at things. We studied New Age theories and philosophies, learned about chakra energy points, and healing by thought control. We learned how to repeat many different 'mantras' and were led to believe that this act would enhance our life in some way. We learned about spirit guides and how they would help us. We learned that everyone has an aura, and that there

70

are many different colors of them. We even practiced learning how to 'see' someone's aura. One individual in the group desperately wanted to experience out of body travel, so we dedicated several evenings for this purpose. I did not find that to be a particularly comfortable exercise, however, as I was never able to fully let go of remaining mentally in the present. The meetings were very interesting and I seemed to be acquiring much information about a subject that I had known nothing of before, although parts of it were somewhat parallel to the spiritual beliefs I already had. Occasionally I would get a little whisper of a feeling that this was not quite one hundred percent what I was looking for, but at least I was busy doing something. I convinced myself that the little something that was not quite right was merely that I was mourning the loss of my father, and wanting to be closer geographically to my mother, grandmother and siblings. I continued to dabble in meditation for about a year, and my life stayed busy with family, work, friends, and general daily activities.

July 10, 1989 was a beautiful day. I had spent a pleasant morning at my house with our neighbor's daughter, a college student. I was considering taking some college courses, so she had come over to show me how to correctly read the college course booklet for the coming year and give me some basic information and pointers about how to apply for college and what to expect. After she left, I mulled over what she had told me, and felt sure that this is what I wanted to do. I had to go to the bank that morning, and since it was a beautiful day, I decided to take advantage of it by walking downtown and enjoying a breath of fresh air while I ran my errand. I was thinking about our morning's conversation and feeling excited about embarking upon this new direction in my life as I walked to the bank.

Being as how it was just a normal, beautiful, day and I was running errands, I was totally blindsided by what happened next. As I walked around the corner of one brick building and entered one end of the outdoor mall area, I suddenly stopped in my tracks. Right there in front of me the heavens opened, and I saw - and felt - a vision of God's glory.

Some visions are apocalyptic. This means that the vision – a symbolic picture that is seen – vividly conveyed an idea. This was definitely, without a question, a vision!

Where the familiar hills around the town should have been, my eyes saw what can only be described as a multitude of people, a massive crowd, so huge that it faded away into the distance, into the sky, all around as far as the eye could see: I could see my beloved father standing right beside Jesus (instinctively I *knew exactly* who that man was – He was Jesus). Jesus was standing to the right of a huge white pillar of light that appeared to come down from the sky. Both of my grandfathers and one grandmother, who had all passed on, were there also, beside my father and Jesus, blending in with this massive multitude of souls. I *knew* that at least some of these souls were my ancestors who had walked on earth before me, and now they were mingled beautifully into this gigantic multitude before me.

I felt at one with the vision! I was spiritually connected to each and every one of them, and each and every one of them was spiritually connected to me.

Jesus, as well as every single person in the vision, was gazing lovingly upon me with kind, warm eyes, and smiling!

I was immediately encompassed in a majestic feeling of elation, an extreme happiness, with such intensity that mere words can never do it justice. I had never before experienced such a profound emotion, and doubt that I ever will again, as long as I am here on this earth. It was exactly three days later that it became clear to me that the feeling I had experienced was God's pure, unconditional love for me, rather than elation or extreme happiness. God had chosen to freely pour out His love on me, and to let me receive this gift of His blessing while I did not even know Him.

My eyes immediately welled up with tears because of the overwhelming emotion I was experiencing. It took several seconds for my eyes to clear, and when they did, the vision was gone. I could do nothing but stand there in the mall square and weep openly and emotionally. I do not know how long I stood there. Perhaps it was thirty seconds, or maybe a minute or two.

Slowly, reasoning crept in, and I frantically thought, "What on earth am I going to do and say if someone sees me standing here crying, and asks me why?"

When I looked around in panic, there was not another living soul moving about in the entire mall area. A surreal peace firmly settled over me. It felt as though God had gently put His hand over me and the mall area, and made time stand absolutely still while I mentally eased back into the normal.

I have never before or since experienced this stoppage of time. Time literally stood still.

Very, very slowly, time began to move again. Not where I was, but in the distance, far away from where I was standing. What seemed to be minutes later, I saw someone slowly walking away from the post office at the far end of the mall. A few more minutes after that, someone else strolled along somewhat nearer to me, towards the grocery store, although still some distance away. However, no one moved about anywhere near me. Little by little, I felt the movement of time slowly encompass where I was standing, and everything returned to normal.

When I felt ready, I went into the bank and conducted my business. I felt positively jubilant, and wanted to throw my arms into the air and shout out loud what had just happened to me, to no one in particular, just to let it out to anyone and everyone who would listen! Wow, wouldn't *that* look good! I controlled that thought, and refrained. Then I wondered if my eyes were still red from crying. What would I say if someone asked me why I was crying? But it was a wonderful cry, a happy one. I remember thinking that I had just experienced something so phenomenal and miraculous that surely my face must be glowing. I was very tempted to ask the bank teller if my face actually *was* glowing, because it felt like it must be. I also wanted to ask her if I looked different, because I *felt* different. However, I would be at a loss as to what to say if she answered that yes, I did look different, so I chickened out from asking the question.

Besides, if she agreed and said that I did look different and then asked me why, surely I would begin to weep again as soon as I tried to speak and explain.

No matter! ...I felt exceptionally marvelous!

As I walked home, my body felt unnaturally light, as though my earthly body had been shed, and only my spirit was 'walking'. I felt as though I was simply floating along, propelled by legs that were moving back and forth in a walking manner, but had no weight to them whatsoever, and were not even touching the road beneath me. In fact, I felt so elated that I remember thinking that if I actually did started to run, I would surely become air born and be able to run on the wind. (I wish now that I had tried it.) But if that did actually happen, how on earth would I ever explain *that* to anyone who saw me? After all, it was in the noon of the day, and there were people around!

For the rest of the day, I felt positively elated!

Acts 7:55, 56
"But Stephen, full of the Holy Spirit, gazed steadily into Heaven and saw the glory of God, and he saw Jesus standing in the place of honor at God's right hand. And he told them, 'Look, I see the heavens opened and the Son of Man standing in the place of honor at God's right hand.' "

Chapter 9

Opposing Forces

Immediately, that very same night, another exceedingly strange phenomena occurred. I had just fallen asleep, and was woken by an extremely deafening sound. The noise was violently loud, and I instantly likened it to what can be best described as a massive chain saw roaring right beside the bed next to me, where my husband and I were sleeping. The noise was distinctly coming from my side of the bed. Even though the roar had awakened me, my husband appeared to be sleeping very soundly. This was extremely unusual, because he has always been a very light sleeper, and intensely alert to noises in the house, much more so than I was. Yet tonight, he appeared to not even hear the earsplitting noise in our bedroom, and was just lying beside me, continuing to sleep very soundly as if nothing unusual in the least was happening.

Suddenly, I began to feel an excessive tightness in my chest. Physically, it felt as though my rib cage was being inflating from inside my body and swelling to an extremely enormous proportion. It was as if my heart and the organs inside of my rib cage were expanding rapidly. Mentally, it was impressed upon me that my 'soul wanted to get out and be free of my body' to soar around and experience the 'out of body travel' that we had been talking about at recent meditation meetings.

Instinctively, I *knew* that all I had to do was simply open my mouth and this intentional, physical action would *give the permission that was needed* in order to *'allow'* my soul a gateway from which to escape out of my body. My spirit would then go on the most fantastic 'out of body' adventure that one could ever hope for. It would far surpass any expectations or experiences that anyone in our meditation group had ever spoken of or encountered.

Something about that transpiration in the dark night, however, felt awkward and uncomfortable in some inexplicable way, so I did not open my mouth to "allow" my soul to leave my body. However, the feeling of mental pressure to do so remained for several minutes before the noise slowly died away and the sensation left. Throughout the entire time, I never once had the urge to open my eyes. Eventually, the night resumed back to silence and stillness for me.

I did not know then that this was the beginning of a very long period of spiritual warfare in my life.

2 Corinthians 11: 14
"... Even Satan disguises himself as an angel of light."

Chapter 10

The Importance of Sharing Information

Wow!!!! I have just had a vision of my father standing right beside Jesus!

The majestic feeling of euphoria!

Lucky, lucky me!

Now what?

Am I supposed to *do* something now?

I should probably be doing *something*, but *what?*

On one hand, this vision was way too big a deal to merely keep it to myself. It was a positively surreal experience which literally 'came out of the blue'. Never in my wildest dreams could I ever even make up something so vivid, majestic, and surreal. On the other hand, what was I supposed to *do* about the fact that I had just witnessed a heavenly vision? Nothing else had changed around me.

I knew of only one other person who has had a vision of Jesus. He was a Doukhobor man originally from my hometown area in Manitoba, and had been an acquaintance of my parents. We had met several years earlier and became friends in the isolated northern town of Kitsault. I had not known him before we met there. He once told me that my father had helped him to quit drinking when he was younger. Something that my father had said to him seemed to 'sink in' at a crucial time in his life, and he was able to let go of the hold that alcohol had on him.

After I got to know him better, he confided to me one day that he had seen Jesus. When he shared that information with me, it seemed to be so important to him at the time, I was embarrassed to realize that I was not able to make so much as one teeny weeny intelligent response to his comment. I remember not knowing what to say, but thinking that I probably should say something to be nice and polite, and perhaps even positive.

I had never heard of anyone actually seeing Jesus before. I could tell that my friend was entirely sincere in this conversation and that he wasn't lying, but I didn't have a clue as to how to talk about something like that! The only way I had heard and used the word before was as a swear word. I assumed that Jesus was connected to God and heaven somehow, because they were all lumped into very effective swear words when one had to make a point, but that was about the total extent of what I knew about Him. I truly didn't know a single thing about Him.

When the time had felt right for my friend to share in confidence with me about what he had seen, our conversation probably went something like this:

He, displaying caution, quietly said to me, "I saw Jesus one day."

There was a long and absolute silence on my part. *What* did he just say? Where'd that come from? I couldn't possibly have heard him right.

"What?"

"I saw Jesus one day."

I did hear him right. What could he possibly be talking about, anyway, and what on earth am I supposed to say to *that*?

"What do you mean, 'You saw Jesus one day?' "

"I *saw* Jesus one day."

Silence. I'm thinking.

"Jesus?"

"Yeah, Jesus."

"You just *saw* Him?"

"Yeah!"

"You just *saw* Jesus?"

"Yeah."

There is a long silence on my part while I process this information.

"Where was He?"

"In the closet."

"What do you mean, 'In the closet'?"

"He was *in* the closet."

Silence.

"Where were you?"

"In bed. Sleeping. I had just fallen asleep. I woke up and there He was, standing in the closet."

Huh! I'm thinking.

"You just woke up and He was *standing* there?"

"Yeah."

"Just standing?"

"Yeah."

"Was he doing anything?"

"No."

"He was just standing there?"

"Yeah!"

In my mind, I imagined the scene. There seemed to be no rhyme or reason for an apparition to appear to someone and then just stand there... let alone in a closet.

"Did He say anything?"

"No."

"He just stood there and didn't say anything?"

"No."

Well! What was even the point of him telling me this if this is how it ended? I surely didn't have anything else to add to this conversation. If Jesus didn't do anything or say anything, then I had really nothing else to say about that situation. However, being ever so polite and wanting to say something positive since my friend had shared something rather special with me, I most likely said something pointless like, "Well, that's nice," while inwardly feeling like I had no clue what so ever about what he was talking about.

I do remember that he talked about it for a while, but I do not remember that there was a specific point to his story. I also do not remember it making much of an impact on me, other than I thought that he must be a very special person in some spiritual way in order to have seen Jesus. If he mentioned to me how it made him feel at the time, I do not remember. I also don't remember what was going on in his life at the time, if he even told me that. It was a rather common occurrence amongst our people to see spirits, but for someone to see Jesus was certainly something new for both of us.

Now here it was, years later. I thought about my friend's vision of Jesus as I compared it to my own. They were oddly similar in the sense that He did not speak to either of us, nor actually do anything specific, other than He smiled at me. Maybe Jesus had smiled at my friend, too. I honestly do not recall if my friend said that He smiled at him or not. I wished I could talk to my friend now. I certainly would pepper him with a few more specific questions now than I had when he had told me about his vision years earlier. He had recently passed away, though, so this was no longer an option.

Still, I had no clue whatsoever as to why Jesus chose to show Himself to my friend or to me, but it must be important. Anyone who has their own swear word has *got* to be important! Interestingly enough, when I think about it now, when I swore in the Russian language, I never used any words associated with the Heavenly realm. Nor had I ever heard any Russian words used in this manner while I was growing up, although I knew plenty of others! It was only in the English language that the words God and Jesus and Christ were used for emphasis in swearing.

As days and weeks passed while I thought about this awesome experience, I could make no sense of it. Trying to figure it out seemed virtually impossible without discussing it with someone else. By keeping it to myself, I was getting nowhere, as I only had my own point of view to work with, and I knew absolutely nothing. To make matters even more confusing, although I knew nothing about Jesus, during the vision it had been specifically impressed upon me that it was definitely Jesus who was standing beside my father. There was absolutely no doubt in my mind as to that fact.

Like it or not, I would have to talk to somebody about this. Maybe then I would have an idea as to what I should do about it, or at the very least, what it meant?

It made my husband extremely uncomfortable when I mentioned the incident to him, so it was not something that we could talk about. I very carefully analyzed the personalities of my friends who were closest to me at that point in my life. We never discussed anything even remotely connected with God, let alone Jesus. The topic simply never came up in our conversations. Because of this, I assumed my friends were all non-Christians like me, with the exception of one.

I had a wonderful back yard neighbor at the time. I must have gotten to know her and like her as a friend and a neighbor long before I discovered that she was a Catholic. I am positive that if I had known that she was a Catholic when I first met her, my prejudices at the time surely would have led me to be extremely wary of her, and I would have been very careful not to get too close to her. By this time in our lives, however, we were good friends and coffee buddies, and I thoroughly enjoyed her company. She openly went to church very regularly, even though her husband never went with her. I rationalized that she should know something about Jesus, since she went to church all the time. So I thought I would ask her.

I mulled around the idea of approaching her on the topic of the vision I had seen for quite a long time, and then when it seemed right, I very cautiously mentioned my vision to her. She did not seem shocked or concerned, and in general, she seemed to think that my vision was a good thing. Even though she could tell me no reason as to why this happened, or what I should do about it, her positive reaction to this bit of news made me feel better, even though I still did not understand it. I was confident that at some point in time, someone would be able to explain what had happened to me.

Little by little, over time, I did manage to talk about it with all of my closest friends. One by one, when the time felt right and I felt enough courage to do so, I spoke to each one of them, every time hoping for an answer as to what it could possibly mean. I had a deep down internal gut feeling that it must have *meant* something.

Everyone's reaction was different. Most of the conversations went very much like the one I had with my friend years before, only this time, I was the one on the flip side of the talk. They were the ones with the blank looks on their faces. Most of my friends were merely puzzled by unusual phenomena such as a vision, although a few shared their own spiritual beliefs with me at the time. Only one made an inappropriate, joking comment, and although I was too polite to get up and leave the table where we were sitting, I made a point of never mentioning it in her company again.

I rapidly discovered, however, that I could not speak of my vision without getting extremely emotional and teary-eyed every single time, an action that discouraged me from wanting to even talk about it. I did not like getting tears in my eyes and a squeaky voice every time I spoke of it, but I had absolutely no control over the fact that I became extremely emotional and began to cry as soon as I spoke the words out loud. I simply could not help myself.

Doukhobors are known as 'Spirit Wrestlers.' That was the derogatory label given to them in 1785 by Archbishop Ambrosius of the Russian Orthodox Church, who intended it to mean that they were struggling against the Holy Spirit. They gave it their own interpretation – "We are Spirit Wrestlers because we wrestle with and for the Spirit of God." They turned away from violence and coercion, choosing to struggle for a better life by using the spiritual power of love. In my family, however, this spirit world was not explained or discussed as being directly connected to Jesus. I do remember my grandmother on the farm trying to tell me about a 'hreestos', (the Russian word for Jesus). I did not understand many of the words she was using, so therefore I got very little out of our conversations. And I never did really grasp the meaning of the word 'hreestos', either. It was many years later that I heard that word in Russian and realized that it even meant Jesus. But my grandmother did try to teach me something about Him when I was younger.

Over the next several years, I also told my mother and each of my brothers and sisters of the vision, one by one, in person, while we visited the prairies on our holidays. I felt that since our father was there in the vision, they had a right to "know where he was" in the spirit world, so to speak, since I had seen him obviously alive and well, smiling and looking happy. After all, they were missing him, too. During these talks with them, I probably put more focus on the fact that our father was okay, and now in a place with his own parents, my mom's father, and all our relatives who had gone before him. My conversation came more from the point of view of confirmation that, yes, he and all our other relatives before him are all alive and well in the spirit world. All was exactly just as we believe!

The only confusing part was seeing our father standing beside Jesus.

I found it extremely difficult, however, to speak about this to my dear, loving mother, who has always been my role model, a lady whom I admire and have a great deal of respect for. I knew full well how she felt about churches, and Jesus is a word definitely associated with the church. I almost felt mean telling her about it, because in my mind, listening to my words would bring back many negative memories of our past to her: memories of the family's and neighbor's horrific stories of torture, starvation and oppression; heartbreaking memories of being a little girl and seeing her grandfather's back, deeply scarred from whippings; all results of the Doukhobors being persecuted by the church and czarist army in the old country.

Still, I felt that I *had* to tell her. It could not have been easy for her to hear what I had to say. She listened quietly as I spoke of my vision. When I was finished, she thoughtfully reflected for a few moments about what had been said, and then in her loving, kind, and gentle way, she said, "No one can explain why these things happen."

She was definitely correct about that. Even though it had been an extremely difficult, one-sided conversation to have with her, I knew in my heart that I had done the right thing by telling her.

My youngest brother was the last one of my siblings that I told about the vision. That was just the way our visits at home worked out. When I finished that conversation with him, a very peaceful feeling washed over me. It was almost as if a closure of some sort had taken place. Only *now* was I finished – I told everyone in the family of my vision. That night I had a dream. In my dream, my father appeared to me and gave me a very warm, loving smile. The dream clearly conveyed a message that he was pleased because his wife and all of his children now knew of the vision in which he was standing beside Jesus.

Luke 15:3-7

"So Jesus told them this story: 'If a man has a hundred sheep and one of them gets lost, what will he do? Won't he leave the ninety-nine

others in the wilderness and go to search for the one that is lost until he finds it? And when he has found it, he will joyfully carry it home on his shoulders. When he arrives, he will call together his friends and neighbors, saying, 'Rejoice with me because I have found my lost sheep.' In the same way, there is more joy in heaven over one lost sinner who repents and returns to God than over ninety-nine others who are righteous and haven't strayed away!"

Chapter 11

The Right People in My Life

Little by little, I began to feel less satisfied with going to the meditation meetings. I also began feeling that they were 'wrong' for me somehow. I could not really explain how or why. It was just a feeling. Here I must point out that in the living room at the house where we used to meet to meditate, there were only two main pictures on the wall. One picture was of Jesus, and one picture was of someone else who was a spiritual leader of some sort. I do not remember his name, or what 'religion' he was supposed to represent, although I had been told. Even before I experienced the vision, whenever we were gathered together in that room, I would feel comfortable when I looked at Jesus' picture, and less comfortable, even a bit unsure when I looked at the other one. I had the feeling that Jesus' picture represented something good. I was not sure what the other picture represented, but it did not give me the same feeling of comfort that Jesus' picture did. After the vision, I began feeling that Jesus should not be compared to or put on the same level as the other fellow whose picture was on the wall, although I had no concrete reason as to why I felt that way. I just did.

In the meantime, life was getting more complicated. Our daughters were teenagers, and their problems and issues were getting more complex. I hoped that we were raising them right, but many times I would second guess the decisions we had made as parents, I wasn't sure if we had used the best approach in dealing with certain issues. I worried about them and our family life a lot, in general. There did not seem to be a written set of rules anywhere to follow as life's choices got more difficult. We merely muddled through in the best way we knew how, trying to do what was best for our family. Sometimes, however, I would spend a fair bit of time worrying about things.

One night I had another dream. In my dream, my husband and I were sitting in a large group at some sort of a counseling session. Each person was given a list of about eleven or twelve items. Some of the items on the list were: job, money, family, security, and several others that I cannot remember. The assignment was to analyze the list and then to individually write down what our priorities are, in order from that list. We were to rate number one as to what was the most important thing in our lives at the time, with number eleven or twelve being lowest on the priority scale. Every separate item, however, was relevant by itself in my life. In my dream, I looked at the list hard and long. I spent a very long time carefully considering each one and switching items around on the list several times until I had them in an order with which I was completely satisfied.

As soon as I leaned back in my chair, relaxed and entirely confident that I was finished, I immediately heard a firm, loving voice, *"You have to put me in number one. Then I will help you with all the rest."*

I had very comfortably put God in eighth or ninth place on my list, out of eleven or twelve.

I had absolutely no idea how to "put Him" in number one place. Everything else on the list was tangible and real. He was not. How on earth was I supposed to even do that?

At this time in my life, I began working with a new coworker who had just been hired. He was a very energetic, conscientious young man, with a delightful sense of humor. He was very easy to talk to and was also very open about being a Christian.

He was not familiar with Doukhobors, so I was more than happy to tell him about my background and what our/my beliefs were all about. It all seemed to be new to him. He did not really agree or disagree with what I said. He just listened. Sometimes he would ask me a question or two. Whenever I asked him about his point of view in regard to whatever we happened to be discussing, his answer almost always included something that was written in the Bible relating to that particular issue. I began to think that his parents had not taught him as much as one single, solitary thing apart from the Bible. He never, or at least very seldom, referred to his parental guidance and upbringing. He almost always related to the Bible. I felt sorry for him. It seemed that he had not learned very much from his family, as I had. If I did not quite understand what he was trying to explain to me, I would ask more questions to clarify specific points, and he would patiently explain and re-word his answer until I finally did understand. His answers always made sense to me, but so did my beliefs, which I felt very strongly about. There seemed to be two ways to look at things that made sense now. It seemed that the Doukhobor way of life was not all that dissimilar to his Christian beliefs as to how people should live.

When I began to talk to him about the meditation group and all my newly found worldly knowledge about New Age beliefs, our conversations took on a whole new meaning. Again, he reverted to what the Bible had to say about any single, specific issue that I had learned about. Sometimes what I believed from New Age teachings was similar to but not exactly in agreement with what his Christian thinking was.

When he began to quote word for word from the Bible about an issue, I rapidly learned that even though New Age phrases used words similar to those in the Bible, their meaning conveyed an entirely different message. I was going to have to be very careful and think about the way in which things were worded. He mentioned several times that the scariest and most convincing type of lie is one that has a tiny grain of truth in it, and therefore it could appear to be more convincing than an outright lie.

His explanations from the Bible always made 100% sense to me all of the time. My New Age beliefs and ideas were not always that consistent. I hated to admit it, but my conviction about New Age philosophies varied somewhat in regards to the amount of sense they made. When I mentioned what I had learned about charkas, energy and mantras, all that he said was he 'didn't know anything about any of that sort of thing because none of those words were in the Bible'.

Finally, here was something I could teach him! I eagerly tried to impart my wisdom on this matter to him, but he really did not appear to be very interested. He was polite enough not to tell me to stop talking, but he clearly did not believe that there was any value of truth whatsoever in what

93

I was telling him. Not even a little bit. He seemed totally content with his beliefs in the Bible alone. When I would get frustrated with him during our discussions, and start to get pushy by trying to convince him about the meaning behind some of those words, and how to apply it to our lives, he always had the same answer, "If it's not in the Bible, it's not true!" Period! Discussion over!

He was simply not interested in any of the knowledge that I was willing to share so eagerly with him. He was not nearly as anxious to listen to what I had to say as I was to listen to his point of view. In fact, he was practically narrow-minded about these new ideas that I presented to him, yet he seemed to be such a nice guy in every other way. Talk about stubborn! I found that to be rather puzzling.

So I figured I would try some other tactics on him. I would ask some really hard questions about life, like something about the afterlife, where we go when we die, our spirit, why bad things happen to good people, ghosts, that sort of stuff. If he could not answer something immediately, he would simply say so. Then he always said that he would go home and look up what the Bible had to say about it, and come back to me with an answer in the next day or so. He always came back with an explanation that made perfect sense. I could never seem to stump him. Not even once. I tried, though, really hard, day after day, relentlessly trying to make my point.

During these 'discussion' periods of ours, he very often repeated another phrase (possibly hoping it would sink into my head so I would quit tormenting him): "The answers to every question you will ever have are in the Bible. You just have to look for it in there."

What a stubborn mule he was acting like!

Without realizing it, I was very slowly coming to admire the fact that he was solidly grounded and absolutely unshakable in his beliefs. He absolutely never wavered from what the Bible had to say about anything we ever talked about. It seemed to be important in all aspects of his life. Maybe these religious people weren't so bad after all, at least some of them. He seemed pretty nice. My Catholic back yard neighbor and I got along swell, too. I guess it is true that there is a good person here and there in every single group of people. I seemed to have stumbled across a couple of nice religious folks.

Little by little, I stopped going to the meditation meetings. I was still searching for something, but the meditation meetings did not feel right anymore. It took a long, long time, however, to totally get out from under the hold that the "New Age" beliefs had on me. I remember cleaning out some papers in a cabinet, and holding a file folder of New Age papers, feeling that I could not discard or destroy them, at least not yet, and then putting them away in case I 'needed' them again.

At around this time in my life, my husband and I were invited to an anniversary party for friends of ours that we had known for many years, back in the Yukon days. I had babysat their two youngest children on occasion, and later on, their two oldest children babysat my kids in turn.

The 25th wedding anniversary party was a beautiful, informal affair held outdoors in their huge yard. We were having a wonderful time, surrounded by good friends, excellent food, and nature's exquisite glory in the form of trees, flowers, birds, a wide, rolling river, and beautiful hills. One of the daughters took me over and introduced me to an elderly couple, the local preacher and his wife. Good grief, I had a beer in my hand that I was thoroughly enjoying!

I remember feeling very surprised to see them at a regular anniversary party where alcohol was being consumed and people were smoking, and I even heard some people swearing. I am not sure why I felt this way. Maybe from somewhere in my past, I had the preconceived notion that they were set apart from regular folk in some peculiar, unknown way, and would have absolutely no tolerance for such things. I watched them very carefully at that party. They barely seemed to notice this atrocity. In fact, it did not seem to fizz on them one single bit! I, on the other hand, half expected lightning to come down from the sky and strike solidly in the middle of our party because we surely were not adhering to some sort of important rule here. I, for one, did not even enjoy finishing the one beer that I was drinking when I was introduced to them. I thought that surely religious people only hung around with other religious people, where they could create an atmosphere where there was no alcohol or smoking, so nothing bad could possibly ever happen there. However, here were these two elderly people, appearing to be enjoying themselves thoroughly in everybody's midst, just the same as everyone else.

It seemed like there were many things coming my way that I had to learn to look at differently.

Romans 12:2

"Don't copy the behavior and customs of this world, but let God transform you into a new person by changing the way you think. Then you will learn to know God's will for you, which is good and pleasing and perfect."

Chapter 12

There's A Preacher in My House

Over the next few months, for about a year or so, I would occasionally bump into the preacher and his wife uptown, at the post office or the grocery store. Having been introduced at the party, we would exchange hellos, and eventually go on about our way. They seemed to be very pleasant people. They were old, too... really old! They looked like they had to be at least in their sixties, but they didn't seem too scary to approach, either. Both of them appeared to be regular, nice, old grandmotherly and grandfatherly figures.

I still had my vision on my mind, however, with no explanation for it or why it had happened to me. A very unsettling and scary idea began to formulate in my mind. Perhaps I could ask this preacher and his wife about it? Maybe they might know something?

I could not seem to be able to block the vision out of my mind and pretend that it did not happen. I began to have the feeling that the vision, which I had seen with my own two eyes and felt with more emotional passion than I ever thought possible, had to hold some sort of specific message for me.

Otherwise, why else would I have experienced something so extraordinary?

Life was chugging along as usual, and nothing else had changed except the way in which I was viewing the world around me. I still had absolutely no idea what the vision meant, with the exception that my father was happy and smiling in the place where he was now living, in the spirit world, and he was beside Jesus. I was pleased that my father was now in this good place, together with his parents and grandparents who had gone on before him, and that they were all in the company of multitudes of others. But why was he, along with the rest of the legion of spirits that I had seen, beside Jesus? In my mind, these were two totally separate things.

My curiosity about finding the meaning behind the vision that I had seen was turning out to be stronger than my apprehension and reluctance of being around a preacher and his wife. I cannot stress enough that, without exaggerating, I had extremely serious apprehensions about being around a man of God, a man of the cloth, as was an old saying. It was bad enough to be in a crowd with these people at an outdoor party, surrounded by many others. It was an entirely different thing altogether to be so much as entertaining the horrifying idea of sitting with them, one on one, in private, and talking about something extremely personal. After all, they were special somehow. They were the people that were close to God, and He was way up there!

However, the feeling to have the vision clarified not only persisted but seemed to grow until it was almost an obsession. I could not get it out of my mind. I knew I would never have any peace in my life until this issue was figured out. There was only one thing to do.

One day, I mustered up every bit of courage that I had, in my whole life, and stepped totally out of my comfort zone. I not only stepped out of, but it was so far removed from me, it seemed it was nowhere in sight at all!

I looked up 'Reverend Godfrey White' in the phone book, picked up the phone, and dialed the number. I identified myself, probably made some kind of panicked small talk, and then said that I would like to talk to him some day, if that was at all possible. Secretly I was wishing that he would deny my request. Maybe if I was lucky, he wouldn't be free, and then this misery would be legitimately postponed and I could put it out of my mind for a while, content that I had made a sincere effort.

No such luck!

We set up a time that I was positive my husband would be at work, my children would be at school, and we would have a couple of hours to ourselves. I gave them our house address.

Finally, I would have an answer to the mysterious vision I saw. What a relief it would be to have that issue dealt with. Then I could just get on with my life, living normally like everyone around me, like I too, had been doing merrily before all of this started.

As the day of our meeting approached, I did not dare tell anyone, not my husband or my friends, that I had invited a preacher over to our house. I would meet here privately with them, get some answers to my questions, and no one else would ever have to know that they were here in my house. There was not really any actual harm being done, after all. They were only coming over so that I could ask them some questions. It seemed simple! However, I felt like I was betraying myself and my family somehow.

The two separate worlds that I seemed to be living in were getting smaller. There was the regular, obvious world in day-to-day life with my family and friends where everything was normal and out in the open. Then there was the spiritual, unseen world about which I was secretive, hiding my attempts to try and make sense of the vision in which I saw my father's spirit standing next to Jesus.

The anticipated day of our meeting arrived. I had baked something to be hospitable, (Doukhobors are very good at that), made sure the house was clean, made tea and coffee, and anxiously awaited their arrival. Finally, I was ready! Their car pulled into our driveway.

I nearly fainted dead away!

What on earth was I thinking, inviting them here? Here it was, broad daylight, and their car, not just any old car, but a *preacher's car*, was sitting in my driveway. I hadn't thought this through at all!!!

Absolute sheer panic filled me. Maybe I could ask them to park in the back yard. We had a big, solid fence around the back. No one would see their car if it was parked inside the back yard.

No, that would just be mean. I couldn't do that. They really seemed to be nice, elderly people, a lot like my own grandmothers and grandfathers, in fact. They might take offense to being asked to park in the back yard, hidden from view. But surely they would understand why when I told them. After all, they were supposed to know everything.

What if my neighbors saw their car in my driveway and said something? What on earth would I say as to why they were here? What a mess I had gotten myself into! One of our neighbors was surely going to mention to my husband that the preacher was here, with his wife. As if we were on friendly terms, or something. That would be something else I'd have to deal with! What had I done? The only thing that I could hope for now was that their rather ordinary looking car looked generic enough that it could belong to anyone visiting me. Yes, that was it. It could be someone else here. No explanation would be necessary, but if someone did ask, I could just make up a fib and say it was someone else, maybe even from out of town.

It felt as if many minutes had passed since they had pulled into our driveway. Where were they? I looked out the kitchen window as inconspicuously as possible, and there they were, taking their sweet time, just getting out of the car and closing the car doors, very, very slowly. Well, they were both quite old, right? Maybe they could not move any faster. What was I thinking, anyway, inviting them here? With the speed they were moving, surely someone in the neighborhood would see that it was, indeed, them, getting out of their car and coming into my house. My only hope was that they would get inside my house as fast as possible, and that their rather ordinary car was undistinguishable.

I politely waited inside. I certainly had no intention to go outside in broad daylight and welcome them where my neighbors could all see us. What could possibly be taking them so long? It was only a few quick steps from the driveway to the front door, and they still hadn't even gotten to the front door yet. The more my thoughts ran rampant, the quicker my panic was beginning to rise again. I looked out the window intentionally this time. No more pussy footing around. They'd better get in here!

I could not believe my eyes. There they were, standing on the sidewalk, not moving at all, but instead they were standing absolutely still, bent over, happily admiring my colorful columbines that were in full bloom in the front flowerbed, like they had all the time in the world. For pity's sake! The whole town would know they were at my house if I didn't get them inside soon. So much for a fib that someone else was here.

Eventually, after what seemed an eternity to me, they did make their way the few more steps up to the front door. Respectfully, I allowed them the time they needed to knock on the door, and I tried to act nonchalant when I opened it to welcome them inside. What I really wanted to do, however, was to propel them inside at top speed before anyone saw them. It would not look very good, however, if I hustled them inside rapidly. I closed the door behind them as quickly as I could without appearing impatient, and hid them safely inside. I was finally able to calm down and stop being in a panic. They still had to leave later, mind you, but I would worry about that then.

I put on a front of casual hospitality, but inside I was mortified. I found them very easy to talk to, and even felt quite comfortable in their presence, right from the very beginning of that first visit, considering what and who they represented.

There was, nevertheless, one little aspect of our conversation that I found rather annoying. Even though I specifically asked Reverend Godfrey some questions, sometimes it was his wife, Betty, who would answer me. He seemed okay with that. I was not. For two reasons: one, he was the preacher (Reverend, it said in the phone book), and therefore he was specifically the one I wanted to talk to. And two, I had preconceived notion in my mind that only a man who was known as a man of the cloth would know about the heavy-duty religious stuff I was building up the courage to ask about. His wife was surely just a woman, like me. What could she possibly know that would be of any help to me? Our husbands were merely in different lines of work. After all, all preachers were men (to my very limited knowledge), and therefore they must intuitively know more about these things than women did. That is why they were the preachers, and not women. Women had dreams, and interpreted these dreams in a manner to help others. That was our female role. My sheltered, loving upbringing in one very specific culture was making me see things through a very narrow scope.

I did not get around to asking them about the vision on that first visit. It just seemed too heavy a topic to just heap on someone so early in our time together, as I also needed to "feel them out", so to speak, and be sure that I was totally comfortable with them being the ones I would ask for help with interpreting something as important as my vision. I felt that I wanted to get to know them a little better, first. We had several more visits at my house, and not a single neighbor ever mentioned anything, much to my relief. I even began to relax in their presence and concentrate somewhat on whatever it was that we found to talk about on those first few and awkward visits.

One very important fact that surfaced relatively quickly in our time together was that this very same Reverend and his wife, who were sitting here at my kitchen table, had spent several years in the ministry at Grand Forks, B.C. It was a geographical area with a very high Doukhobor population. In fact, their oldest daughter was married to a Doukhobor man there.

Lucky, lucky me to have found these exact two perfect people that I needed right now. I couldn't believe my good fortune!

They were totally familiar with my background beliefs. That fact in itself was a monumental relief for me. These guys actually understood me and knew where I was coming from. I could be myself around them, although I still put on my best front for them. Nothing I said seemed to surprise or even fizz on them in the least. I even accidently swore once or twice in their presence, as this was my natural way of speaking at the time. When I caught myself after this happened, I suppose I half expected them to get up and walk out, or some unseen natural disaster to strike me down immediately. At the very least, they should reprimand me for swearing in their presence, out of respect for who they were. However, nothing happened!

Our visits were quite normal in every sense, just like my visits over coffee and goodies with anyone else. All of my exaggerated fears about speaking to someone 'religious' had been totally unwarranted. Besides, they had seemed perfectly comfortable talking to me right off the bat.

After several visits, when the time seemed right, I mustered up every bit of courage that I had, and told them about the vision I had seen. I was surprised that I was still so emotional while talking about it, after all this time. I had to struggle to keep the tears from welling up in my eyes when I spoke. In a way, I half expected them not to believe me. After all, I was not really convinced that any of my friends and family (except maybe my Catholic friend), whom I had spoken to this about, believed a word of what I had said when I had finished telling them. Maybe these two would be no different.

I was in for a very pleasant surprise. They not only believed me, but they seemed to be sincerely delighted and very pleased to hear about my vision. They were actually interested and open to talking about it! This was the most enthusiastic response I had received yet, after mentioning it to someone. What a major relief that simple fact was. I *had* been right in feeling led to talk to them about it. Reverend Godfrey said he would pray about it and get back to me.

I was rather surprised with his reply, as I had expected an answer right away, then and there. After all, didn't preachers have some sort of a direct line to God? The next time that we met again, neither he nor his wife Betty mentioned it. Nor was it mentioned the next time, or the time after that. I was beginning to feel that my vision must have been forgotten about, but I was too polite to bring it up again. I didn't want to remind them about something that was so important to me, as if to do so would be insinuating that perhaps they were getting old and forgetful, although that exact thought did cross my mind more than once.

Approximately a month later, much longer than I thought it would take, Godfrey came back to me with these pivotal words: *"Thelma, Jesus is telling you, 'Keep your eyes on me!'"*

He assured me that he had prayed about it very long and hard, and he was positive that was the exact message he was to pass on to me.

My first thought was, 'Okay, that's easy, no problem'. Seconds later, that smug thought changed to one of 'How on earth am I supposed to do that?' It is not like Jesus was someone who was right here and I could just follow Him around, watching Him and picking up important pointers here and there. I had expected an answer that would entail me perhaps in doing something nice once or twice, whatever it may be, and then go back to living my life exactly as I had been living it before. You know – simple, easy, uncomplicated, and just like everybody else. Betty and Godfrey, however, did not seem to be at all baffled by this message that they delivered to me.

It took many more questions on my part and several more meetings with them for me to learn exactly how I was going to do that, to 'keep my eyes on Jesus'. More realistically, it probably took that long for me to accept the idea that this was going to be a journey in which I had to change not only my ways of thinking about things, but also some of my ways of acting, and daily habits, as well, such as swearing and gossiping, to name only two issues that came effortlessly to me at that time. This was not going to be as easy as I had hoped and thought it would be, let alone be a simple cut and dried path.

One thing that Reverend Godfrey and Betty did was speak to me a lot about was my view of and my belief in God. I did believe in a higher power, but up until then, I never actually thought about God specifically being *the* highest power. I suppose He could be. It was impressed upon me that God was the *only* One, and under Godfrey's and Betty's gentle guidance, I did come to believe this to be true. God/Jesus was not only at one with the spirit world that I was comfortable with, but He was also above it, bigger than it. The spirit world was all a part of His creation.

I am sure that they offered me a Bible, but I already had one. I had bought one for myself years ago when my daughters were in kindergarten and the first grade because I enjoyed reading and had taken a notion that I wanted to read the Bible. I did read it from cover to cover, like any book, but although parts of it were interesting and entertaining, other parts were extremely confusing and did not make sense. Some parts were just way too 'out there' – people walked on water and did not sink down, people got thrown into a furnace and did not get burned, people were thrown into a lion's den and did not getting eaten alive, nine people were raised up from the dead, and many, many more wild stories. It was sort of like an Aesop's book of Fables, in a way. I kept it in my top drawer. I could not help but notice, however, that Reverend Godfrey often would 'back up' his explanations with a sentence or two from the Bible, here and there.

Surprisingly, it always made sense. Maybe his Bible was different from mine.

Reverend Godfrey and Betty also spent a fair bit of time trying to explain the Holy Spirit to me. No matter how they worded it, I just simply could not seem to comprehend and really understand exactly who the Holy Spirit was, and how He was associated with God and Jesus, and much less, with me.

At this point in time, in my everyday life, I was an active reflexologist, and one of my clients was a lady who was bedridden with illness. Her condition responded well to reflexology, and I worked with her three times a week. She couldn't pay cash, so we developed an interesting barter system. Sometimes she would pay me with fabric, because I sewed, once it was a wooden salad bowl. It was always a surprise to me what I would be going home with for payment, but more importantly, her medical condition was responding positively to reflexology.

As a rule, I would go to her home for these appointments. Her husband would let me into their house, show me to her bedroom, and then leave while I worked on her feet. One particular day, I had just gotten started working on her feet when her husband came into the doorway and planted himself there firmly.

In a louder voice than I was used to hearing him use, he announced, "I had a dream last night and I have to explain the Holy Spirit to you!"

You could have knocked me over with a feather. I had never spoken a word to these people about my personal life, and now here he was, out of the clear blue, standing in the doorway, boldly and loudly telling me who the Holy Spirit was, and how and why He was connected to my life. The reflexology appointment lasted for about forty five minutes, and he spoke the entire time. Just as I was completing the work on his wife's feet, he appeared to wind down his explanation about the Holy Spirit to me.

Before leaving the room, however, he boldly declared one more message for me, "And one more thing… you have to bring the Word of God to your people!"

With that, he turned and walked out of the room.

His wife just looked at me and quietly said, "I don't know what got into him. He never talks like that."

His mission was accomplished, and I actually had a very clear understanding as to who the Holy Spirit was. The very idea about considering I would have to "bring the Word of God to 'my people'" was completely baffling. How in the world would I ever be able to do such a thing? I didn't even live amongst 'my people' anymore.

Not only that, who were these Christians that they just seemed to pop out of the woodwork, when least expected, and hit the nail right on the head with a perfect explanation about something that they had absolutely no way of knowing I needed in the first place? No wonder people were wary of them!

I mentioned this to Reverend Godfrey and Betty the next time that I saw them, although I felt rather guilty doing so. They had spent so many hours answering my questions and explaining things to me that I felt awful that my understanding of the Holy Spirit came from someone else. They, on the other hand, were thrilled, and did not take it personally in the least. The most important thing, they explained, was that I understood. It did not matter who did the explaining.

At this point in time, Reverend Godfrey and Betty were also discussing with me the importance of the physical act of being baptized. They patiently explained to me, most likely many times, that Jesus himself had been baptized as an example of a physical commitment to a life dedicated to God. By now, I was beginning to get the distinct impression that 'keeping my eyes on Jesus' was going to require more than a couple of good deeds or a weekend or two of some sort of special service. I was feeling ready to make a commitment to Christianity, because what I had experienced so far was all good. Baptism would apparently be the next natural step. Although I did not seem to be able to comprehend completely why this was important, I trusted that if they said it was important, then it must be so. Naturally, I wanted to share this marvelous experience with my daughters, so I asked them if they would like to be baptized with me. My oldest daughter, who was sixteen years old, accepted. My youngest daughter, then fifteen years old, declined.

On March 3, 1991, my oldest daughter and I were baptized in the little local church by Reverend Godfrey White. My wonderful friend and backyard Catholic neighbor was my sponsor. My daughter's very close Catholic friend and neighbor was her sponsor.

Now that my daughter and I were baptized, I thought that I was 'there'. I was done, finished! The only problem was, however, that I still did not seem to know too much about Jesus, and my vision was specifically about Him. As well as our talks with Reverend Godfrey and Betty had gone, one on one in my kitchen, or sometimes in theirs, I began to realize that in order to best learn about Jesus, I would benefit from a group setting, where I could learn about God, Jesus, the Holy Spirit, the Bible, and how it all comes together. Many Bible teachings seemed to center around people who gather together regularly to learn from each other, encourage each other and help each other. The extremely disturbing part about this realization to me was that, as far as I could tell, the only place that people met regularly to learn about God was in a church!

1 Thessalonians 5: 12, 13
"Dear brothers and sisters, honor those who are your leaders in the Lord's work. They work hard among you and give you spiritual guidance. Show them great respect and whole-hearted love because of their work. And live peacefully with each other."

Chapter 13

Church??? Really???

Horror of all horrors! My life had now come to this!

Even *I* could barely believe that I was entertaining thoughts about actually going to church. I was comfortable in my life. Even though I had experienced this recent bout with unrest relating to the vision, I was okay with everything else. And now, as if I couldn't just let things be peaceful and leave well enough alone, here I was, considering going to church.

However, getting back to my vision, realistically, I could only 'keep my eye on Him' if I could figure out how He related to the everyday world around me. Unfortunately for my nice little comfort zone, no one else in my life at this time seemed to be too interested in accompanying me on this journey to discover Jesus.

Try as I might, I could not think of any way to get around the disturbing fact that the only place I was going to learn about Jesus so that I *could* 'keep an eye on Him' was by going to church. Believe me when I say that was a scenario I wanted to avoid wholeheartedly. I thought about every angle possible. There seemed to be none! Reverend Godfrey and Betty probably could sense my resistance but they never pushed me. They most likely had no idea of the depth of my fears hold on me.

How could I ever leave my house on a Sunday morning and physically walk or drive to church and just saunter inside? We're talking about *me* here! It was bad enough to sit and talk at home with a Reverend and his wife, but it was another thing altogether to start going to church in public, in a small town where everyone knew you. I was sure that I would have to live with questions and comments from everyone I knew.

I was also very aware about how 'regular people' talked about 'church goers', and it was not flattering in the least. Negative phrases I had heard and continued to hear many, many times came to mind, phrases like:

"Hypocrites"

"They do what they want all week, then ask for forgiveness on Sunday, and go back to living however they want for another week. What a joke."

"Churches are just after your money. They're the biggest scam going."

"People who go to church are all weak and need something to lean on."

"Those people can't face life, so they hide behind the church."

"The Bible is just a book written by men. Anyone can write a book. Who would be so stupid as to believe it?"

"Churches are no different than any other cult. They just want to control people."

"The Bible was written so long ago that it has nothing to do with today's world, and yet people still believe it. Some people believe anything that is told to them."

"You should see so and so – he goes to church all the time and then steals when he's at work. Religion is a farce."

"They just brainwash you there."

"The Bible has been rewritten so many times that the original message has been lost long ago."

When I stopped to think about it, I really had never heard anything positive said about church or the people who go there.

Life was clearly divided into two sides: the 'us' and 'them'. My friends and acquaintances may start to think that I am one of 'them' if they see me publically going to church just because I need to figure out something in my personal life, which I certainly was not about to share with anyone. Everyone I knew seemed to be happy. At home, I felt comfortable discussing these issues with my teenage daughters, and they assured me that they did not have a problem with my going to church.

I thought about my beloved mother. How would I ever be able to tell her, and what could I say to her, knowing that she was always so dead set against churches and preachers? I felt as though I would be betraying my entire family, as well as the Doukhobor sect in general, by turning my back on the lifelong traditions that helped make me who I am. After all, Doukhobors do not go to church, so I could not be both things. I could not begin going to a church and still remain true to my Doukhobor roots. In my mind, it was impossible for the two to mingle.

But at the same time, I still had a fierce uneasiness in my soul, a yearning for something to fill a void I could still feel in my life. I could not just pretend it was not there. I felt very torn in two directions. One side was the present life I was living, where my husband, my children, my mother, my grandmother, my friends, my brothers and sisters and their spouses, nieces and nephew, cousins, aunts and uncles, and my entire background belief system were solidly in place. On the other side were this surreal vision and a friendly little elderly couple, the preacher and his wife, and answers to all the questions that I seemed to have, gently encouraging me how to learn to 'keep my eyes on Jesus'.

I do not know how long it took for me to muster up the courage to actually physically go to church. It was a move that took every bit of courage that I had. Reverend Godfrey was the Anglican minister of the interdenominational church in Logan Lake. It was explained to me that he took one service a month. The other Sundays of the month were filled by a United minister, a Lutheran minister, and sometimes visiting ministers, which included the Gideon's, Salvation Army, and Presbyterian, to name a few. But everybody who was a member of the Logan Lake Christian Fellowship was welcome to attend all of the services. Suddenly it all seemed to be very complicated. I didn't even know what those words meant.

I do remember, though, leaving the house with mixed feelings. I was still apprehensive and nervous, even though I had made my decision to go there. There was also still a seed of doubt as to whether or not this is what I really should be doing. When I did walk into the church, I was very surprised at how many people I knew there. Many were faces that I recognized as customers who came into the bakery where I worked, and others were acquaintances from around town. Everyone was very pleasant, greeted me happily, and then went about 'doing their own thing'. Not one single person asked me why I was there. Somebody gave me a book of some sort, and a piece of paper with stuff written on it that I was to 'follow'. Then I went into the inner room where my daughter and I had been baptized. I walked to the very front pew directly in front of the stand where the minister would be standing to speak from, and sat down. This would be perfect. I could see everything, and would surely be able to hear everything from here. Surprisingly, no one sat beside me. As people came in, they seemed quite content to sit way in the back. I could not believe that people weren't scrambling to cram in to the front pews. I thought this was very strange.

Betty was one of the musicians who played the organ or else the piano for the church services. I honestly do not remember who else played the music those first few Sundays that I attended. I was very astonished to discover that two teachers who had taught my daughters in elementary school were musicians there also. That was a surprise. I didn't even know that they went to church. They actually seemed to be just normal, regular teachers when I had met them in the classroom. It comforted me to have them in church with me, somehow, and the music itself soothed me.

When the service started, although everything was strange to me, I felt amazingly relaxed, considering my prior apprehension to coming here. As the minutes passed by, I even began to enjoy some parts of the service. At one point, I am not sure exactly when, a dreamlike feeling of extreme peace washed over me. It seemed to reach deep down, right to the very core of my being. I felt tears of happiness start to well in my eyes, and it was impossible for me to stop crying quietly.

It was mentally impressed upon me that *this was it – I was home at last!*

What a wonderful, peaceful feeling that was. What a relief! I had finally found out where I needed to be. *This* is what was missing from my life!

I probably went to one service, mulled it over for a couple of weeks, and then went again, only now it would have been somebody else's service, not Reverend Godfrey's. I do remember attending one service at which someone that I knew only casually seemed genuinely happy to see me there, and very helpfully insisted on helping me be seated. She proudly let me to a seat right beside her in one of the very back pews. I remember feeling slightly annoyed, because I could not see anything from back there, and probably would not be able to hear anything, as that was not where I wanted to be sitting. I was there to learn, and I would learn better being up front where I could easily see and hear everything going on. Out of politeness, I did sit through that service in the back pew, but I was not happy about it.

On one hand, being nice and polite to a point where it was making me unhappy in this new experience was not proving to be a good idea. On the other hand, I had the notion that a lot of people who go to church regularly have a specific place that they like to sit every Sunday, and I did not want to offend anyone by arriving earlier than them and accidentally sitting in their spot, either. No one seemed to want to sit in the front pews, so that was probably a safe bet as to where I should sit, and that is where I wanted to be anyway.

I probably discussed this dilemma with Betty and Godfrey. Over time, I began to feel very comfortable discussing all my concerns associated with churches and Christianity in general with them. Since I had no church experience what so ever, I needed to be able to talk to someone about both large and small issues. They were both very nice people and I always felt that they were extremely sincere in whatever we talked about. No matter how trivial my 'problem' was, they helped by giving me wise advice in a manner that still allowed me to make the decision regarding the issue. The fact that they were old was comforting to me, too, because I was raised to believe that our elders have a lot of wisdom to share with anyone younger, if we choose to listen. I felt extremely fortunate to have found them.

Eventually, I decided that once I began going to one church regularly, I would have to commit to it wholeheartedly and deal with the consequences of negative Christian 'labels' as they came my way. There were not too many choices in Logan Lake for churches. However, I was encouraged to try them all to see where I felt the most comfortable and seemed to 'fit in' the best. I went to a Roman Catholic service, and that did not seem to feel quite right. All the Russian swear words I grew up hearing associated with Catholics fairly rang out loud in my head the entire time I was there. I also went to a Baptist service, they met at the Elementary School gym at the time, and that did not seem to feel one hundred percent right, either.

During this period in time, I came to a very marvelous realization. Other than the one hour spent inside of the church one day a week, the rest of my

119

life merrily went along as usual. This change over was going to be much more on a mental than a physical level. Up until then, a lot of my concerns had been about what other people would see and think about me. Nobody seemed to care in the least! I had worried for nothing. Physically, life went on as it always had: my husband went to work, I went to work, our children went to school, we cleaned the house, bought groceries, went out to visit friends or had friends over to our house, mowed the lawn, did laundry, went fishing, took holidays, and carried on with every day chores and activities as usual. Many times when I was feeling overwhelmed with mental changes, I took great comfort in daily routines such as baking, sewing, gardening in the summer, or cross country skiing in the winter. These normal everyday routines confirmed that life would go on as usual in many ways, and I just needed to find a balance between the two. It was a monumental relief to me when I realized that!

It did not take me long to decide that I was most comfortable at the Logan Lake Christian Fellowship, which met at the Logan Lake Community Church.

This would be my church! I had made up my mind.

One Sunday morning dawned, and I went to my chosen church for the first time, seriously and purposefully knowing that this is what I wanted to do and where I wanted to be doing it.

There, I got the surprise of my life. A relatively small man about the same size as my father, with dark hair similar to his, walked into the sanctuary through the side door at the front, carrying a guitar. He casually strolled over to where the piano was standing, and began to strum cords, filling the room with beautiful guitar music that I had been so familiar with from my youth. I could not believe my eyes or my ears. Here was a man playing his guitar in church! I thought churches only had pianos and organs. As the sound of guitar strings being strummed filled the sanctuary, I felt myself slowly slipping into a very peaceful and comfortable place. When this gentleman began to sing, I got another fantastic surprise. It was a song that I knew, one that I had heard my father play and sing many times while I was growing up. I remember wondering why he was singing that particular song, since I had a preconceived idea in my mind that only some sort of special songs called hymns were sung in church, and 'Amazing Grace' was about the only hymn that I knew. This song wasn't that one, but now was not the time to worry about that. I just allowed the music to fill my soul, and enjoyed drifting to a place of absolute tranquility, one where my memories included my father singing and playing his guitar as he had done so beautifully for years for us kids.

Immediately, I felt entirely at peace and extremely joyful about being here in church. Tears filled my eyes as my very spirit experienced 'coming home'. This is exactly where I belonged. I felt a sense of completeness that I had never before experienced.

When the guitar music ended, a very friendly looking little lady in flowing robes came out of the side door and made her way to the front. A woman preacher! She introduced her husband, the guitar player, and immediately I had to wrap my head around the role reversal of this couple at the front of the church. She made me feel at ease instantly, however, as soon as she started to speak, and I found that her role as preacher was extremely fitting

121

as to the way in which she was speaking and presenting herself. She simply looked so comfortable up there, just as if that were where she belonged. Her face absolutely radiated peace. During the rest of the service, I enjoyed every single song that her husband played on that guitar.

During the service, many times I heard specific words spoken casually out loud that I had only ever associated with swearing before this. No one else seemed to even flinch at the use of those swear words in this rather Holy place. It seemed like no one else was concerned in the least about the language being used, although I must admit, the words were inserted into sentences that made me believe that there must be another meaning to them other than the meanings I had been familiar with.

Another thing that caught me off guard was when they came to a part of the service in which to pray. There were kneelers in front of us, and I automatically expected everyone to lower the kneelers, and kneel to pray, like I had seen so long ago at our friend's Seventh Day Adventist Church. I did not hear any kneelers being brought down, so looked around, and no one was kneeling to pray. They just sat in their pews with their heads bowed down and their eyes closed. I did not want to be different, so I did not kneel, either, although it did not feel quite right to me to pray just sitting there with my head down. I remembered a song that my father used to sing when he played his guitar, and part of the chorus went this way:

> 'On your knees, you are taller than trees
> You can look over heartaches and pain
> When my faith is gone, to my knees I will go
> Growing stronger, and taller than trees.'

Many years later, a most wonderful friend gave me all the words to this song and also told me exactly how to find this song on my computer. I will always treasure her for this touching act of kindness that was so very meaningful to me.

I felt a strong personal need to kneel while praying. Otherwise, I was just sitting there. I could sit anywhere, anytime. I had fully expected that everyone in the church, who was physically able to, would kneel to pray. Not only was I shocked that they didn't, but I desperately felt that I, myself, wanted and even *needed* to kneel to pray, on some spiritual level deep inside of me. But I also wanted to fit in with everyone else, so I did not kneel.

I immediately discussed this problem with Reverend Godfrey and Betty. They assured me that everyone was free to pray in the manner in which they felt most comfortable, and if I wanted to kneel, to just go ahead and do it. No one would judge that movement in one way or another. The next Sunday that Reverend Godfrey took the service after our discussion, he specifically said, before the prayers, for everyone to pray in the manner in which they were most comfortable, whether it be sitting, standing or kneeling. I was very relieved to 'have permission', so to speak, from the minister, so I very contentedly lowered the kneeler and knelt to pray. For me, it felt 100% right in my heart, and I have continued to do so regardless of how others around me are devoting themselves to prayer. No way is right or wrong. We are merely encouraged to lift our voices to God in prayer in whatever way is right for each individual.

Over time, I gradually became accustomed to the different services at the Logan Lake Christian Fellowship Church every month, and became comfortable in going regularly every Sunday, unless we had other plans as a family. I tried hard to be sensitive to the needs of my family, and to keep a balance between my personal needs and desires for Christian education and fellowship and my need to maintain the regular, normal way of life with my family that had been our lifestyle before I began to travel down this separate path.

Matthew 18:20
"For where two or three gather together as my followers, I (Jesus) am there among them."

Chapter 14

Trials

Now that I had taken the terrifying step of moving into the unknown, there was a great peace in my spirit as I began to learn about Christianity. Much of what I learned at church was about how to treat others and how to live in harmony with everyone around me, with respect for every single human being. It was the very same information I was raised with in my own family as a Doukhobor. Many of the words and terminology were different, and that's all. The two worlds that I was combining were not so different, after all, much to my relief.

However, there always seemed to be something new to learn with regards to Christianity. I loved that! Just when I thought I fully understood one concept, thinking I 'was there' and that I 'knew everything' about a specific topic, something slightly different would pop up that was closely associated with it, and that led to a whole new set of questions from another angle, and an entirely new concept. At first, I found this to be extremely annoying as well as very tiring, because I wanted to 'know everything'. I rapidly realized that I would probably *never* know everything, and this was going to be a life long journey of learning. It took me a long time to accept that as a   good thing.

Going to church and listening to the stories in the Bible being explained was easy. Many of them carried a message that I could relate to. Gradually it was impressed upon me that I should at least try to begin applying what I was accepting as a truth at church into my everyday life. There was nothing specific saying exactly that, (or if there was, I just wasn't 'getting it') but there seemed to me that several services in a row, by different preachers, hinted about the same things. I took it that those 'hints' were meant as something we should at least try to do. For some strange reason, I felt guilty if I pretended to ignore what I should be changing when the opportunity arose to do so during the week.

For starters, I would have to cut out swearing. Even when I was good and mad, apparently now swearing was not acceptable. How would I ever blow off steam if I couldn't swear? Also, I should try to tell the truth *all* of the time. Up until now, I thought that little white lies were okay if they did not actually hurt anyone. It was a struggle to apply what I learned in church to my regular life, and I caught myself frequently being aware of my shortcomings.

My struggles, however, were not mine alone. From the time we had been baptized together, my older daughter was also affected, but in a very different way. Several weeks after we had been baptized, a long weekend approached. My daughter had gone to a friend's house to work on a homework project. She was in a habit of always coming home on time, and on this particular evening, my husband and I were concerned because she was approximately twenty minutes late, and this was highly unusual for her. We phoned her friend's house, and they seemed surprised that she was not home yet, as she had left in plenty of time to walk home and arrive when expected.

Almost immediately after I hung up the phone with our friends, she walked in the door. Instantly, I could tell that something was very wrong. She seemed disorientated, and appeared disheveled. Her long hair was messed up and her face was unusually pale. I asked her what was wrong. She said that she didn't remember much of what happened, except that as she was walking home on the dark path near our house, something struck the back of her head very hard. She was late arriving home because she had been lying on the ground, unconscious, in the dark, merely yards from our doorway.

Immediately, I heard the words, *"Satan is mad because he lost her!"*

Where did that come from? And what did that have to do with anything, what so ever, at all? I had my daughter to tend to, and never gave that voice much more thought at the time. My husband instantly phoned the local RCMP detachment (the Royal Canadian Mounted Police). They arrived immediately, rapidly assessed the situation, and called for a tracking dog to come in. They worked late into the night tracking her attacker. Her injury was not extreme, but the situation was. She healed from the physical injuries quickly, but mentally, the incident shook up our entire family for a long time.

The next year, on a long weekend in the spring, our oldest daughter was hurt again. Only it was worse this time. She and many other teenagers had been at a 'bush bash'. Bush bashes were very common, and still are, in our area. They are a party out in the woods where the local teenagers gather on weekends to cut loose. An argument erupted at this one, and it ended with my daughter being struck very hard from behind, on the lower part of the back of her head, with a big stick. We were told later, at the hospital, that if the blow had been two inches lower, the force would have broken her neck and could have either paralyzed or killed her.

As it happened, someone was at the bush bash with a vehicle, which is not always the case, and someone there was also trained in first aid and recognized the severity of the injury. They brought her in immediately to the local diagnostic and treatment center, and she was sent out by ambulance to the Kamloops hospital. A specialized ambulance and attendants were dispatched from Kamloops to meet half way to ensure proper treatment.

She was hospitalized for three days with a severe head injury. For about two weeks after being released from the hospital, her speech and concentration were affected. Many times during the day, she would lose her train of thought part of the way through a sentence, and was unable to finish. Worse still, psychologically, she did not enjoy being in crowds anymore, even if the group were all friends and school acquaintances. For a long time afterwards, she only felt comfortable in crowds if her back was to a wall and no one was behind her. I found this to be extremely upsetting, and hoped that she would not suffer long-term effects from the trauma.

Two years after that, the fourth year after she and I had been baptized, she was in her final year of high school. One night I had a dream. In the dream, my husband had been out hunting and shot a moose. As I walked over to where he stood beside the moose, I could see that this moose was absolutely massive. It was bigger than any moose I had ever seen, and as I walked towards it, it became more enormous until it was almost as big as a house. There was a great deal of raw meat exposed where my husband had started to cut it up. I was thinking that this was really great because now we would have meat all winter from this massive moose. When I woke up, I was amused by the size of the moose in my dream. I also felt that surely something really good was coming our way because the moose had been so very big. I phoned my mother and told her about the dream, excitedly waiting to hear what she would have to tell me about her interpretation. She was much better at interpreting dreams than I was. She was quiet for a moment, and then said that it was not very good to dream about raw meat. She did not think it was good at all.

Not long afterwards, late one night in a long weekend in the spring, we received a phone call and were told to go immediately to the hospital in Kamloops. Our daughter had been in a car accident, and was hurt very badly. Our youngest daughter was out with friends at the time, and we made two phone calls to try and locate her so that she could come to the hospital with us. She was at neither place, and we knew we had to leave immediately, so we reluctantly left without her. Just on the edge of town, there she was, miraculously standing on the road, in our headlights, all by herself. We stopped the van and picked her up. I asked her how she just happened to be standing there in the road at that exact time that we needed her. She replied that she was at a bush bash, and suddenly just knew that she had to get out to the road. I reflected on her words for a moment, and thought that it was all a bit unreal how that happened, but the incident was quickly forgotten. I was just thankful we were all together.

Upon arrival at the emergency ward, we were told that our daughter was on life support, and that she would not survive the night. A very kind nurse unlocked an office door and said we could use that room for privacy. Then she told us to go and say our goodbyes to our daughter, one by one. I remember feeling furious at the nurse for saying such a thing. Who did she think she was to tell us something like that? I do not remember in what order we went, and I do not know what my husband nor my youngest daughter said when they had their time alone with her. I only remember feeling totally numb, as if we were all moving in a very slow nightmare of a 'dream' that could not be possibly real in any way.

When it was my turn to go, I slowly approached the hospital bed behind the closed curtain. There lay my beautiful daughter in that bed, looking so small. Her eyes were closed.

I didn't have to say goodbye. She was just sleeping. There was machinery and tubes everywhere, some of them quite loud, and there seemed to be a lot of lights and lines on screens. It seemed to be a very busy place that I had no understanding of. I did what I was told. I said the word out loud.

"Goodbye, sweetheart," or honey, or whatever pet name I was using for her at the time.

That just didn't feel right. Goodbye? How could I just say goodbye to her? How could I possibly go on with my life if she were not in it? I couldn't. That would be absolutely impossible! There was no way that I would be able to get through even one single day if she were not in our lives. How could this be happening? I just could not say that and mean it, no matter what the nurse wanted.

So, I told her words that *I* wanted to say, instead. I encouraged her to live. Those words were easier to say, and I really meant it. I started to tell her to something to the effect of 'Hang in there. Don't give up. We are here for you. Fight. Don't give in. You'll get better. You're young and strong. You can make it. Don't quit'. The nurse just looked at me with sympathetic eyes, and did not say a word.

I walked back into the little room where my husband and youngest daughter were sitting. The overwhelming feeling of helplessness and misery hung like a heavy black cloud in that tiny space. They both had their heads down. To the absolute core of my being, I felt so sorry for them. Their silent despair broke my heart. Even in my state of shock, my heart was already totally broken.

I got the feeling that I should pray. I had, by this time, begun going to Bible Study classes, and heard Betty and the other ladies pray out loud. I had never done it myself, though, so I really didn't know exactly how to pray. I had just listened to others pray. However, being a new Christian, I felt that prayer was something that I should be doing right now, and that might give me hope. My husband and my youngest daughter looked full of despair, and that made me feel very badly for them. I wanted to reach out, join hands with them in a circle, and pray out loud for our beloved family member that we each had said goodbye to. I also wanted us to pray for each other, for strength to get through this. But neither of them was open to Christianity, so I did not ask them to join hands with me and pray. As I look back now, I wish I had just simply taken each of their hands in mine, and said a prayer out loud, anyway. It may have given them some peace at the time, whether they believed or not.

Instead, I just quietly sat down, bowed my head, and talked to God in my mind, as best as I could, considering how desperately hopeless I was feeling. My prayer started out with pleas for God to help her, to make her better, and not take her away from us. We would surely all be totally devastated without her. Speaking just for myself, I would not be able to resume life without my daughter. Judging by the emotion in the room neither could my husband or my youngest daughter, either. I pleaded for His healing hands to touch her, and make her well. He could do that. He could do anything. He was God!

"Just make her well. Help her to at least breathe on her own. She isn't even doing that. She's lost way too much blood. Please, God, anything you want. Just name it."

I tried to strike up a bargain with God. If He made her well, and if I ever came into any money, I would spend some of it to install some stained glass windows into the little chapel at the hospital so that it would have more of a church feel to it, like the little chapel in the Meserecordia Hospital in Winnipeg, where my father died. The little chapel there was positively beautiful, and it was such a peaceful spot. At present, the little chapel at the Kamloops Hospital was just a plain, small room, with not much of a resemblance to a church. There was a Bible in there, though. I had gone there when she was hospitalized before, when I was feeling overwhelmed with the turmoil that a parent feels when their child is in intensive care. My mind came back to the present, and then I felt bad, thinking how would I ever find the money to put in a stained glass window in that little chapel? I should not make bargains with God that I could not keep, especially if He did happen to come through on His end. No, that was not the way to be praying right now, either. Trying to bargain with God just did not feel right anyway. In my state of shock and inexperience as a new Christian, I did not even know how to pray or what to pray for.

A Bible verse I had come to learn popped into my head. It was a favorite of mine ever since the first time I heard it.

'Be still and know that I am God.'

Be still? That was impossible. I had a million thoughts and emotions running rampant through my mind at lightning speed. I was experiencing absolute mental chaos. However, being 'still' seemed to be a good idea. I would try to do that. I gave myself a stern talking to!

"Get a handle on your panic and be still. Okay. Try to do that. Breathe. Breathe. Take deep, slow, intentional breaths.

Focus!

Stop the chattering hamster on the wheel in your head and just be still.

'Be still and know that I am God!' That's what the Bible says. *Do it!"*

133

Deep breath in.

"Empty your mind."

Deep breath out.

"Empty your mind."

Deep breath in.

"Empty your mind."

Deep breath out. "

"Just breathe. Nothing else! Empty your mind of panic. Breathe!"

A new idea slowly and quietly formed itself in my mind. I did not like it, though, not one little bit. I tried to ignore it.

I couldn't!

The idea became clearer and stronger regardless of my resistance to it. I not only did not like it, I absolutely and thoroughly *hated* it. This was definitely not the thought that I wanted taking up space in my mind.

I had to give her up.

I had to stop pleading to God about what *I* wanted Him to do. I had to stop trying to make deals with Him so that the results would be what I wanted. I had to acknowledge Him as our creator and loving Father, and let Him be God. I had to relinquish all control over to Him entirely, instead of me trying to control the outcome of this tragedy by thinking and saying positive thoughts and phrases and bargaining with Him. I had to trust Him in this situation that I had absolutely no control over.

Okay then. I would do it that way. My way wasn't working anyway.

Quietly, in my mind, I spoke to God again. I took a different approach.

My talk with God (was this praying?) now went something along these lines: "Heavenly Father, I give my loving daughter to you. I give her entirely to you. Her body is broken, we have had to say goodbye. If it is your will to take her home to you at this time, then so be it. She was yours before you lent her to us, and she is yours still. She always was. I can do nothing. I am totally helpless and can do nothing to help my daughter. Let your will be done, Lord. Not mine. You know how much we love her and want to keep her here with us. However, I give her to you. Totally and entirely, she is yours. Thank you for the wonderful years you let her be with us. I give her to you. She is yours, all yours. Let your will be done. Thy will be done! (Yes, that was a direct phrase I had heard before – 'Thy will be done', so I'll use that)'… Thy will be done, God!"

Now I was finished my talk with God in a manner that felt right to my heart. Rationally, however, I fully expected an immediate nervous breakdown as a result of 'giving up on' my daughter.

Amazingly, the very opposite happened. Slowly, a tiny measure of peace crept into my being. Only now, way deep down in my soul, did I feel as though I had done the right thing. I felt positive, as I had given her to God. I had never before taken this approach as a solution to a problem, small or large. This must be what it means in the Bible when it speaks of 'giving Him my burden'. I did not really understand what that meant before. This was the first time I had actually sincerely and honestly given Him my entire burden in prayer.

Whether or not my prayer had anything to do with what happened, I will never know. I like to think that it did. Her broken body sparked some sort of change that compelled the medical staff to begin working with her as if there was a hope of her surviving.

Our world had changed overnight. For the next three days and nights, we never left the hospital. We ate there, tried to sleep on the chairs and benches there, and stayed beside her bedside while she was in a coma. I prayed for her when I was at her bedside and when I was trying to sleep in the chairs of the waiting room outside of the intensive care unit at the hospital. When I needed a change of scenery, I prayed for her when I went into the little chapel at the hospital. It could still use some fixing up to look more like a church. Sometimes, even though I felt that my prayers were very inadequate, I would feel as though God had heard me, and I would momentarily feel a semblance of peace for a few seconds or maybe even a minute or two, until my worrying took over and I got upset again.

Sometimes I felt that I should be praying with someone else, because I remembered that somewhere in the Bible I had read a phrase that began "Where two or more are gathered in my name, I am there..." I felt that perhaps my prayers would be more efficient if I had someone to pray with me, but I did not, so I just continued to pray by myself, and hoped that I was being heard. I also prayed for my husband and my youngest daughter throughout this time, as their worry and grief was astronomical as well. Praying not only gave me a certain small measure of peace in a predicament where I could do nothing else for my family, but it turned out to be something positive that I could actively do in a negative, helpless situation where I could really do nothing else at all, in a physical sense. My worrying would not change anything, and only drive me crazy in the process. When I focused on specific words in prayer, I seemed to be at least somewhat focused on something positive, and that was a much better head space to try and stay in.

During the time she was in intensive care in a coma, we were told the extent of her injures: one cheek bone was broken, both collar bones were broken, her spleen had been shattered and required surgery to remove it, she had eight or nine broken ribs on one side, a collapsed lung, her pelvis was broken, and one knee had a torn anterior cruciate ligament. I was overwhelmed just listening to the list of injuries. Every single one on its own needed attention and healing energy. Altogether, the list was totally overwhelming. My heart ached for her. Healing was going to take a long, long time.

I do not remember exactly how long she was in the hospital, but I think it was around two weeks. Every day seemed like forever. My mother and my oldest sister came out to support us and I will always be thankful for that. Truth be told, however, I remember them arriving at the hospital and feeling extremely thankful to see their supportive faces, but beyond that, I barely remember them being there. I am certain, however, that their loving presence and calmness in the situation was of tremendous comfort to all of us.

When my daughter was released from the hospital, we were not at all prepared to meet her needs at home. Thankfully, we had only been home less than an hour when our next door neighbor popped in to see if there was anything she could do to help. She quickly assessed my daughter's frail and sensitive form lying on the couch with no proper back support and cushions that didn't want to stay together. She said she knew where we could get a hospital bed to use as long as we needed it. She left, and within two hours, several local men came in with a hospital bed, and set it up in our living room. What a blessing it was to have that hospital bed for her badly injured body. I was so thankful for these wonderful folks in our small community who arrived with help so quickly. Our living room became an area for the hospital bed, the wheel chair, and her visitors. I felt bad that she had absolutely no privacy whatsoever, especially when her friends popped in to visit, but we also knew this was only a temporary arrangement. It would be approximately six weeks before our daughter was well enough to be able to move back into her bedroom. That must have seemed like an eternity to a teenage girl.

Our days became filled with doctor appointments, medical tests, and a wide variety of physiotherapy treatments. The time it took just to get out of the house to keep these appointments was shocking at first. Every physical movement was a struggle and brought pain to her. We realized we would have to begin getting ready at least a half hour earlier than we normally would. I would have to help her sit up in the hospital bed, position the wheel chair so that she could safely lean her body over it, help her lower herself down, then wheel to the main door. There, she would have to stand up, lean on me while she stepped over the stoop and sat on a chair outside by the door while I lugged the wheelchair down the three front steps. I would help her to the bottom of the steps, where she would sit down in the wheelchair and I would wheel her out to the car. There, I opened the passenger car door; she would stand up and lower herself carefully into the car seat. I would fold up the wheelchair, load it into the back of the car, get behind the wheel, and now we could leave. At the other end, all the steps were repeated again in reverse.

As we kept very many appointments with a variety of specialists over the next several months, I came to realize that I had to entirely trust the doctors, nurses, and specialists whose care she was in. More times than not, I was unable to understand all the medical terminology that they were using. It all seemed to be very serious. I took comfort in the fact that I could see small improvements in her health little by little, and we rejoiced in tiny triumphs.

She was not able to go back to school to finish the remainder of the year, but her friends brought assignments home for her to work on as she felt able to do so, and she graduated in June with her classmates. Her graduation was a very emotional time for me. She insisted on walking on her own, without a cane, for the ceremony. I was furious! That made me very nervous, but by this time she was walking on her own a bit, so I trusted her judgment to step carefully.

One day our younger daughter's friend was over at our house, just hanging out like teenagers do. I overheard her say something to my daughter that made me curious, so I asked her to repeat it. She said that surely our family was going to hate Easter after this. I asked why she would think that would be so. I loved Easter time. She pointed out that in the last four years our oldest daughter had been injured seriously three times, each time on an Easter weekend.

I had not made that connection before. I thought it was odd that our youngest daughter's very close friend would see that so clearly, and point it out to us. Could it possibly be a coincidence? As a Christian, I had come to learn and believe that there are no coincidences in our daily activities.

Easter is a very specific Christian holiday in which our Lord Jesus Christ arose from the grave and conquered death as we know it. It gives every single believer today the hope of joining the Father and the Son in Heaven eternally (where I saw my dad standing beside Jesus), when our time on earth is done. We have one shot at life here on earth, and it is up to us to make it the right choices to make it good. There is no reincarnation and coming back again as someone or something else. This is it. One time only!

Romans 8:26, 27

"And the Holy Spirit helps us in our weakness. For example, we don't know what God wants us to pray for. But the Holy Spirit prays for us with groanings that cannot be expressed in words. And the Father who knows all hearts knows what the spirit is saying, for the Spirit pleads for us believers in harmony with God's own will."

Chapter 15

Tribulations

Less than two months after our oldest daughter had been in the accident, while we were still dealing with many medical issues that were extremely overwhelming, I had an odd and extremely disturbing dream.

In my dream, our youngest daughter came home and she was very badly beaten up. I mentioned to her that we had to call the police, and she ran out of the house saying, "No! No! We can't!"

Then, in the dream the scene changed, and my husband and I were sitting at a 'trial' where she was being charged for something that I knew absolutely nothing about. I had not even been aware that she was in trouble of any sort. All the people in the room physically looked very weird. Each person in attendance was wearing many layers of dark, tattered clothing. They all had big hats hiding very dirty, tangled, matted, and uncombed hair, their eyes were looking either haunted or expressionless. The expression on their faces were unhappy, dull, or else fiercely angry. They were furious about my husband and I being in their midst, and made no pretense of it. Someone scowled at us, then waved an arm to some chairs, motioning where they wanted us to sit down. As more of them came into the room, practically each one made a point of casting a dirty look in our direction, and then sat far away, openly shunning us. We were definitely not welcome in this place.

The most vivid part of the dream, however, was the 'feeling' in the room. It was one of absolute evil. The room itself was dark, with an overpowering sense of extreme foreboding. Although there was an obvious lack of order in this 'courtroom', the 'trial' got underway. I suddenly realized that this is a cult which has a severely strong grip on my daughter. Throughout the 'trial', many different individuals went up to her, where she was sitting alone, and loudly berated her, swearing and screaming into her face. Some even slapped her. My husband and I had to sit several rows behind her, and were not allowed to intervene at all, not physically nor verbally. I was forced to watch my beautiful daughter sit in her assigned seat with her head down, not retaliating at all to the physical and mental bashing that she was receiving.

Suddenly, my gut instinct kicks in and I *knew* that I had to get her out of that evil place and away from all the disturbed people gathered there. I jumped up, ran to her, grabbed her by the arm, and started to run out of the building with her. We did not make it out of there. Now these people are very openly angry with me, and make no attempt to hide their hostility towards me. The trial continued in the same manner as before, and I was starting to panic because the abuse directed at her was escalating. I jumped up again, ran towards her and grabbed her arm, trying, for a second time, to get her out of that evil place. We got really close to the door, but failed again.

By now, the eerie crowd is absolutely furious with me and my interference with what they obviously feel is none of my business. Suddenly, I realize that my own life is in danger because I am interfering with the cult's way of doing things, and now they think I know too much. The crowd wants to kill me to get me out of their way. I became truly terrified for my own life. In reality, never in my life have I ever felt such intense terror as I did in this dream.

I woke up in a panic. How could this possibly be happening right now? Our oldest daughter lay in a hospital bed in our living room with so many severe injuries we had no idea of how long it would take her body to heal, or how much was even going to heal, or what long-term effects she would be left with. Now this dream was insinuating that there was a severe problem already in progress with our younger daughter. We already had literally all that we could handle on our plates. How could we possibly deal with another catastrophe right now?

I had been concerned for some time now about our younger daughter's eating habits, or more specifically, the lack of them. This issue had been the source of many confrontations and arguments between us in the past year or so.

I was about to learn immediately that if someone is leaning towards anorexic or bulimic tendencies, a traumatic experience such as seeing her sister clinically deceased and having to say good bye to her will bring it to a head, and it did... with a vengeance! During this traumatic time, we came to recognize the symptoms of full-blown anorexia with our younger daughter. Unfortunately, it was a medical condition we knew nothing about. We certainly did not know how to help her to deal with it. It was a totally foreign world to us, just as foreign as the intensive care ward was for physical injuries.

During the weeks that we had spent at the hospital, we ate most of our meals downstairs in the cafeteria. I became acutely aware of just how bad our youngest daughters eating habits had actually become. I observed that she barely ate anything at all. A healthy, seventeen year old needed much more food for sustainment than she was allowing herself to ingest.

I felt totally at a loss as to how to deal with this added stressful issue. All I could do was encourage her to eat to keep her strength up. No matter what common sense advice I could come up with, I could see that I was having no influence on her what so ever in this matter. Her food intake was extremely minimal, at best. She was surely bound to get weaker and weaker, and with the added stress of the situation at the hospital, I did not know how long she would be able to cope before collapsing. Then I would be forced to deal with that, and I was already overwhelmed by the crisis of her older sister's accident. That insight made me feel very angry and I remember telling her that she'd better eat something and keep it down because I had no energy left for dealing with this. The most frightening aspect of this situation, however, was my realization that I had absolutely no clue as to how to help someone who seemed so intent on starving themselves.

When my husband returned to work and mentioned the situation at home, someone gave him the name of an acquaintance who had two daughters who suffered with anorexia and/or bulimia. We phoned them, explained our situation, and they kindly agreed to meet with us. This informal coffee meeting at their house opened my eyes to a very troubled world that we were about to enter with our youngest daughter. It was a world she was already immersed in. They told us several incidents that had taken place with their own daughters. Victims of eating disorders suffer from intestinal health problems, low self-esteem, and thoughts of suicide and perhaps attempts to carry them out, mental dullness due to lack of nutrition, and a wide variety of psychological issues that were totally out of my league to even understand, let alone try to fix.

However, the similarities between their daughters and mine in the way they acted, spoke, and felt about themselves left no grey area as to whether or not our daughter had a serious eating disorder. She definitely did. None of these issues appeared to be easy to deal with. However, both the man and the woman talking to us over coffee in their home looked fairly relaxed at this point in their lives, while they calmly answered our questions and spoke of many trials they had been through with their own daughters. Just seeing how calm and normal they were now made me feel as though there was a glimmer of hope for my own sanity in this situation.

Because this couple had gone through the local medical system mostly by trial and error, they were able to warn us of ways in which their daughters' situations had not been dealt with in the best way at times. Anorexia and bulimia are extremely complicated, multi-faceted issues that are most effectively handled by an entire team of physicians who are trained specifically in regards to this illness, and who work well together. Such a program was not available in the nearby city of Kamloops. They strongly suggested that the best thing for us to do was to immediately try and get our daughter in to see a specific doctor in Vancouver who specialized in eating disorders, who had organized his own team of professionals. This team had helped both of their daughters tremendously. If left untreated, the statistic at the time was that 30% of victims with this illness die and of the 70% who don't, almost all remain sick with it for the rest of their lives. This was not something we could just ignore and hope it went away. It would not.

We contacted our family doctor for a referral to this specialist and our daughter got placed onto their waiting list. It would be several months before she could even get a consultation to determine whether or not the specialist would be able to accept her as a patient. However, we had to try. After two months, as her eating habits deteriorated and she kept losing weight, I called the specialist's office to see where we were on the waiting list. They did not have her name down. She was not even on it! The letter of referral from our doctor had never made it to the specialist's office. So much precious time had been wasted. More phone calls had to be made to rectify that, but persistence on our part paid off. Finally, she was definitely on the waiting list.

In the meantime, we had many medical appointments to keep in the surrounding cities with a variety of specialists for our oldest daughter's extreme and various physical injuries. Some appointments were in downtown Vancouver, and others were in outlying areas within two or three hours of home. I quickly learned how to pin point a location on a city map, figure out the easiest way to get there, and just drive through whatever traffic or weather I had to deal with that day, regardless of the fact that I was scared stiff of driving in city traffic. This was before the

147

days of GPS where you conveniently enter an address, and a lovely little voice tells you exactly which road to take, which lane to be in, where to turn, and then conveniently delivers you right to the door of your desired location.

During one very low point in my anorexic daughter's illness, I would forcibly make her come with us as we travelled out of town to her sister's appointments because I did not trust that she would not try to harm herself while we were away. I may have been overly cautious at this time, but I had felt better if she were with us as we took many medical day trips. I also remained very alert whenever we stopped our car for fuelling up and buying meals or snacks, and restroom breaks. I felt that she may possibly try and run away, for she was feeling and displaying a tremendous amount of hostility towards me at this time. Our new acquaintances who had gone through this with their own daughters assured us that this was a normal stage of the illness which would come to pass. Their words were a tremendous encouragement to me because I was in totally over my head, dealing with medical issues, both physical and mental, with both of my daughters at the same time.

I found that one of the most frustrating parts of being a mother of a child with an eating disorder was not being able to understand the many varying symptoms, and therefore I did not know what I could do to help. I tried to make sense of all the different issues that make up an eating disorder, but I was never sure what exactly I should be doing. One night I had a dream.

In my dream, a voice clearly told me, *"In her drawer is something that is very significant to her."*

148

It was impressed upon me that this particular 'something' was 'very significant' in an extremely negative way.

The next day, when I was alone in the house, I went into her bedroom and looked around. There were drawers under her bed, full of what I considered to be normal treasures that could belong to any teenager. Her dresser drawers were also full of what I considered to be regular clothes and everyday items that all teenage girls have lying around. I saw nothing, so I looked elsewhere. There were shelves in her closet, also with nothing out of the ordinary in them, just things that teenagers collect and have lying around. I could see nothing unusual, and I certainly could not find anything that even suggested at being a negative influence.

Very soon after I had this dream came an evening in which we were having a rather heated discussion. It was suddenly impressed upon me that now was the time to mention what had been recently told to me in my dream.

I asked her to go to her bedroom and bring out what was so very important to her that was making her feel so angry and frustrated. I was totally out on a limb with this request, and if she questioned me on this, I had no clue as to what to say, because I had absolutely no idea what item that could possibly be, because I had searched her room thoroughly. To my absolute surprise, she got up and went to her room. Now I was really curious, because I had not found anything even remotely suspicious when I had searched through there.

She came out with a stack of magazines, of all things. I still did not see the connection between her illness and these magazines. I knew that she had these teenage magazines and enjoyed reading them, but they did not trigger any warning signs to me of any sort, not when we bought them for her or else when she bought them herself, and most certainly not when I came across them in her room while I was searching for 'something significant'. They were just ordinary magazines that were sold in the teenage section in every grocery store, corner store, book store, and fuelling station across Canada. New ones came out every week.

Little did I know!

She opened one of them up to an article, and began to talk about it. The article was about a young, thin model that was very popular at the time. My daughter knew the model's age, height, weight, and what clothing she had recently worn at which modeling shows, in which country and city the shows had taken place, and how much money that model had made. She knew which school subjects the young lady liked and disliked, how she kept up with 'home schooling' while very seldom actually at home, and how she had to juggle schoolwork and professional work while being in the spotlight, with her every move exposed to the world and her face always splashed on the front of a magazine cover. Then she opened another magazine, and proceeded to tell me many of the same personal details about another famous, young lady who was a model.

I was absolutely flabbergasted!

I let her talk. She talked for what seemed to be a very long time, relaying scores of personal statistics to me about these very skinny young models who she seemed to know so much about. Slowly it dawned on me. My daughter was comparing herself to these world-famous, wafer-thin, professionally made up youngsters, whose jet set lives were publicly written about in a variety of magazines that were available in every little town to every impressionable girl in Canada. She effortlessly quoted fact after fact after fact about many individuals. I remember my mind drifting away at one point, and me thinking that if she knew half this much about her subjects in school, she'd be a straight A student.

When I forced myself to pay attention to what she was saying, I felt myself getting furious, mostly at myself. I had not realized that the innocent act of buying and reading these common, colorful, readily available weekly teenage magazines was having such a profound, negative effect on my daughter's self-esteem. Never once did it even occur to me that there was a problem here. Looking back, I should have been more aware. When our family had gone on a six week holiday across Canada the previous summer, she insisted on bringing a bag full of these magazines. I did not want to, but she was insistent, so we let her. My common sense reasoning was that they were just something she would enjoy reading in the van on the ten thousand mile round trip from British Columbia to Nova Scotia.

But, back at the present moment, my daughter was sitting in front of me with all these 'harmless' magazines in front of her, still rattling off memorized statistics. I knew that this opportunity which had just presented itself was the perfect moment to begin closing at least this one negative aspect of her life. After much discussion, she agreed to burn all

151

the magazines in our fireplace. We lit a fire and one by one, she crumpled up the pages and burned the magazines that were so influential to her. We were up very late into the night, feeding the fire.

While we were waiting to see the eating disorder specialist at the coast, we went through a long period of many months, of what seemed to be one step forward and two steps back. She was hospitalized briefly for an intestinal problem, a direct result of poor nutrition. We introduced meal replacement drinks into her diet, and if nothing else, I felt good about the fact that she was getting at least a little bit of good nutrition every day. I questioned whether or not she kept them down, but at least she drank them.

Just as our friends had predicted, she was hospitalized. Within a few days, I could see that the hospital was the wrong place for her to be (another exact prediction) because her weight kept dropping lower and lower even more rapidly now that eating meals was not even encouraged. When I addressed this issue with the head nurse at the time, she said they were more concerned about what she was thinking, so her food intake was not their primary concern. I disagreed wholeheartedly, and became extremely frustrated because there was nothing I could do to help her, and the professionals did not seem to be on the right track either, as far as I was concerned. So I did the only thing that I could. I prayed.

I prayed for God to take away this illness that appeared to be consuming her, mentally and physically, and prayed for strength for myself to get through this ridiculously difficult period of time with my sanity at least somewhat intact. My calendar was still full of specialist's appointments in different cities, and physical therapy appointments as our older daughter slowly healed from the car accident injuries. There was, however, one bright spot in our lives that I was extremely thankful for. Our oldest daughter was healing beautifully, better than I had ever dared to hope. My prayers for her were being answered before my very eyes.

During this very difficult time in my life, I had developed a practice which gave me some peace amidst the minute to minute, hourly, and daily turmoil. I would light a white candle, and then pray to God regarding specific health issues that were pertinent at the time. I had said many prayers and lit many white candles for my oldest daughter and I had also said just as many prayers and lit just as many white candles for my youngest daughter. It is difficult to explain, but I did not feel as helpless after I lit a candle for and prayed for my children. I felt as if I had *done* something positive. The peace which accompanied these acts was a very welcomed and comforting, regardless of how short lived it may be. Seeing my oldest daughter healing so extensively made me realize that God was with her, and He was the one with the power to heal her at the same time as He was giving me peace.

There came a point in time when my husband and I realized that being in the hospital was doing our daughter more harm than good, so we decided we would go and bring her home, regardless of the fact that her doctor at the time wanted her to stay there. That morning, I lit a white candle and said a prayer which went something like this: "Heavenly Father, she is not getting better there, in fact, she is getting worse, so we are going to go and bring her home today. Please be with us and open the right doors to make that happen. Thank you, Lord. Amen."

Then I went for a shower. When I came out and glanced into the living room, the candle that I had lit for my daughter was out. That had never happened before. Every single time I had ever done that, the candles had always burned down to the bottom.

This particular candle had definitely been lit, and was burning brightly when I had left the room only minutes earlier. It was sitting on the coffee table where I always put my 'prayer candles'. There were no windows open, and therefore no draft in the room to put the candle out. I was the only one in the house at the time. However, the candle was out.

For a few seconds, I just stood there and stared at that extinguished candle, feeling that our well thought out plan for our daughter was not going to happen. I had full faith it had to happen. It was not doing her any good to be where she was, so we left to go and bring her home.

The candle was right. It didn't happen. They would not release her.

We came home very heavy hearted and feeling defeated. Her weight and health were spiraling downward rapidly. Several days later, well past supper and late into the evening, we got a phone call from the hospital. Our daughter was missing! Apparently she had simply walked out on her own.

I felt absolute terror in my heart. She was very young, medicated heavily, and on her own in the city late at night. We *knew* the hospital was not the right place for her to be! We were furious, but there was no time to dwell on that. We phoned good friends of ours to meet us at the hospital. Upon our arrival, she was still missing, so we went out looking for her in pairs. We assigned ourselves different streets and blocks, and checked all the restaurants and bars that were open at that hour of the night, meeting occasionally for updates with each other. Several hours later, at one bar, the bouncer at the door happened to be a young man from our small town. When I asked him if he had seen her, he hesitated before answering me then replied that yes, she had been there. He seemed reluctant to give us any more information, so I explained the situation and why we were looking for her. He then told us that she had come in, had a few drinks, and appeared to pass out. She was in a back room sleeping. As my husband carried her into our friends' car, I could see just how pathetically thin she really was. It was heartbreaking, but at least she was safely with us. We stopped at the hospital, I collected her belongings, and we spent the night at our friend's house in Kamloops. In the morning, we brought her home.

From now on, no matter what happened, we would deal with every single issue that surfaced by ourselves, in the best way we knew how. There would be no more trips to doctors until she could get in to see the specialist that had been highly recommended to us. She was extremely depressed at this time, and dangerously so. We kept a vigilant suicide watch for days, around the clock. I remember making a bed for myself on the floor inside her bedroom, right against the door, so that she would not be able to leave the room without waking me up. My husband changed the lock on the bathroom door so it could not be locked from the inside.

During that fall, she enrolled for home schooling. We all felt that in light of what was happening in our lives at the time, this was the best way to

155

proceed with grade twelve. She had asked to be home schooled for the last couple of years, but we had not agreed until now. This change in approach to education agreed with her totally. All the peer pressure associated with school was off. She graduated from grade twelve a straight "A" student. We should have done that years ago!

Finally, the day arrived when we drove down to the coast to see the eating disorder specialist there to keep our long awaited appointment. For the first time in months, I felt hopeful that help was near at hand. Our daughter would finally be receiving the professional care that would help her to heal from this strange illness that was consuming her. When we arrived at the office, I was hugely disappointed that our appointment would not be with the specialist whom had been so highly recommended to us, but rather with a co-worker of his, someone new to the practice. We were assured that the specialist we would be seeing was well trained in this line of work also, so we agreed to see her.

As soon as we went into her office, she immediately told us that they would not be accepting our daughter as a patient because we had to use the facilities in our local area. I explained that there were none, and besides, there had been no mention of that when I had made the appointment many months prior. After several minutes of our back and forth discussions in this direction, I could not believe my ears. We had waited months and months for this appointment, and now we were being turned away before she had a chance to even be assessed. I was determined that we would get help at this office that had come so highly recommended, and the doctor was equally determined that we needed to go back to our own area. We were each stubbornly holding our ground, and eventually, to make a point,

156

she bluntly said, "We don't have a magic wand here to make things better. You have to see the doctors in your area."

At that point, my daughter and I got up and left her office. I told the receptionist that my original referral was with the other doctor, and that was whom we wanted to see. She, too, tried to discourage me, but I was totally at the end of my rope. I told her that we were not leaving until we saw whom we had originally come to see. She did squeeze us in to see him, and he accepted our daughter as a patient. Finally, for the first time since the eating disorder materialized in our lives, I felt a glimmer of hope that everything was going to turn out all right. She would be receiving the professional help she needed.

Matthew 11:28-30

"Then Jesus said, 'Come to me, all of you who are weary and carry heavy burdens, and I will give you rest. Take my yoke upon you. Let me teach you, because I am humble and gentle at heart, and you will find rest for your souls. For my yoke is easy to bear, and my burden is light.' "

For many months, throughout the winter, my daughter and I drove to Vancouver once a week, every Wednesday, for appointments with the team of specialists. Many times, these trips were far from pleasant. It was a three-hour drive one way, a two-hour appointment, a stop for supper, then the three-hour drive home. Music was an instant topic of disagreement. We had no individual music devices. Right off the bat, she wanted to play her teenage music while we travelled. It was a loud racket that made no sense and annoyed me. I could see after just one trip that this was not going to work. I proposed a compromise: for every hour we played of 'her' music, we would play one hour of my choice. That would be bluegrass – which was equally loud! The music arrangement did not last long. I couldn't stand her music and she couldn't stand mine, so we agreed to not listen to anything. Sometimes she would be very angry that we were making her keep these appointments, so not a word would be spoken during the entire trip. Not there or nor back. Between no music and no talking, it was absolute, blissful silence, except that the mood in the car was so tense, you could cut it with a knife. Anyone who has travelled a distance for any length of time, trapped in the confines of a small, economy car with a teenager who did not want to be there, will know exactly what I mean.

One thing that never changed, however, regardless of the tension between us, was that I knew I could count on her to help me to drive if need be. Both of my daughters inherited my crippling migraine headaches, which I, in turn, inherited from my mother. We all knew how incapacitating they feel. Some Wednesdays, if I was in extreme pain with a migraine headache, I would ask her to drive while I slept. She would gas up when necessary and stop for food and restroom breaks as needed, letting me sleep.

Even under the care of the specialist, she very slowly continued to lose weight over the winter months. As summer approached, she was offered the opportunity to go to an eating disorder camp for six weeks on Gabriola Island, one of the Gulf Islands. The camp was for youth with eating

158

disorders, both overeaters and under eaters. We signed her up for the six week session. I had prayed for guidance in regards to decisions about her health, and this felt right.

Once she left, I lit a white candle and prayed for her daily. Again, it was the only thing I *could* do. The entire situation was out of my hands. I hoped that the same professionals who had helped the family who had given us this doctor's name would also be able to help her. I honestly do not know how I would have made it through that time in my life without prayer. My main reassurance came from knowing and believing the fact that our Heavenly Father loved her even more than I did, so she was in good hands; the same hands that had lovingly held her older sister several times already. I had to hang on to that promise of God's to see us all through.

The camp proved to be a turning point in her struggle with the eating disorder. During her time there, she was diagnosed with and treated for anorexia, bulimia, and depression. Very slowly, over the course of the next few months, life would resume to a somewhat normal state. We began to see glimmers of our daughter's pleasant and vibrant personality that we had not seen for a long time.

Once our oldest daughter had healed from several surgeries, she moved out to be on her own. When our youngest daughter came back from the camp and got full time employment, she, too, moved out to live on her own.

After what we had been through, I was extremely thankful and also even a little bit amazed that the day had actually come that our daughters were both well enough to be able to live independent lives.

Romans 5:3-5

"We can rejoice, too when we run into problems and trials, for we know that they help us develop endurance. And endurance develops strength of character, and character strengthens our confident hope of salvation. And this hope will not lead to disappointment..."

Chapter 16

Live How You Believe

After our daughters left home to begin living independently, I often marveled at the fact that they were both able to do so, after the extreme physical injuries and mental trauma that they had both been through. What a blessing we were given, as parents, to being able to watch their lives get back to normal. I felt extremely humbled that our children's lives had been spared.

My husband and I entered a very quiet time in our lives with just the two of us at home. I came to recognize this as a time of much needed rest. I was mentally and physically exhausted from the previous years. The mundane routine we were in now was a very welcomed change of pace. We went to work, enjoyed our days off, and did more of the same the next week. I could be as busy or as inactive as I chose to be.

It was at this time, when everything was going well and normal again, that I began to slide into a very deep, dark place. I never felt happy, and I had to force myself to smile and appear interested in conversation whenever I spoke to anyone. I stopped enjoying being with my friends and family, and my sleep habits wavered to the extremes of always feeling tired and wanting to sleep, or else being awake for many hours during the night. I did not understand this at all, because for the first time in a very long time, everything in my life was going well. After an intervention from my family, (which I did not appreciate) I agreed to seek medical advice.

I had an awesome doctor who explained it to me this way: "You have been living in a pressure cooker for the last two years."

He diagnosed me with clinical depression, and I began a treatment of antidepressants that I was to take consistently for nine months to a year. Up until I went to see him, I felt that if I prayed hard enough, I would be and should be okay. Unfortunately, the neurotransmitters in my brain did not respond to prayer alone. I hated the stigma attached to being on antidepressants, but they did help. After about two months, I began to feel better so I took myself off the antidepressants. Unfortunately, I slid into depression again. I stayed depressed for quite a while before going on them again. This time I lasted about three months feeling good once more, then I took myself off them again, without telling my doctor. Only after doing this several times and always slipping back into depression did I finally listen to my doctor and stay on them for the length of time he recommended. Slowly, I returned to my usual, normal self, physically and mentally.

My prayer life, however, seemed to be lacking miserably in enthusiasm. I felt grounded in Christianity through regular church services and Bible study, and I still felt very close to God, but my prayers were very dull, at best. I began to think that with the crises in our lives over with, I was straying from God. Although I was not going back to my old habit of looking for answers from fortune tellers, psychics, or analyzing my dreams, I did not feel that God was receiving the enthusiasm and intensity of prayer that I felt He deserved. When I discussed my concerns with my beloved Christian friend, Betty, we determined that because my prayers had been so intense for such a long period of time, now they were equally important, but merely not as desperate as they had previously been. The situation in my life had changed back to that of an average one, and my prayers would logically mirror this situation.

I was still totally sincere in my prayers, just not desperately 'begging' to God during them!

What I was doing was saying regular, normal prayers for a regular, normal life. It was an extreme relief to me to be aware of this fact, and I stopped feeling as though I was 'letting God down', in some way, by not being 'dedicated enough' to have pleading prayers every day.

As a relatively new Christian, I still felt that I had to 'earn' God's love, partly through very sincere prayer. That thought worked well as long as my life was in crisis and my prayers were practically frantic, but now that things settled down, I seemed to be unsure of how to stay close to God. It took me a long time to accept the fact that His love for me was always present, unwavering, and I could never 'earn it'. God's love for me was a gift! Period!

It was a free gift to be graciously accepted and enjoyed by me. This fact was confirmed to me one day at a yearly Bible study held with our Bishop.

His message included a phrase that I will remember always: "We already *know* how much God loves us. That frees us up to love others!"

I found that to be an extremely interesting statement. It would take years, however, before I could actually apply it freely to my own life. First I would have to learn to embrace that love, accept it as a truth, and somehow freely allow myself to enjoy it fully. If my dear friend and mentor believed this to be true, and also my bishop believed this to be true, who was I to argue and dispel such a marvelous truth? After all, they were the 'experts' on Christianity and this particular way of thinking, not me! What a lovely and marvelous freedom accompanied that revelation. I *was* free to love others just as God loves me. The hard part was to get into the habit of putting that into practice.

How very fortunate I was in my life to be in a place where I could hear this loving message and accept it as a truth. How very sad that there are people out there who may never get the opportunity to even hear this marvelous truth.

Ephesians 2:8-10
"God saved you by His grace when you believed. And you can't take credit for this; it is a gift from God. Salvation is not a reward for the good things we have done, so none of us can boast about it. For we are God's masterpiece. He has created us anew in Christ Jesus, so we can do the good things He planned for us long ago."

As usual, it seemed that in my new found knowledge and growth in the Christian faith, I would soon get another chance to put into practice what I had just learned. I rapidly learned, in this instance, that it is one thing to mentally realize something, and another thing entirely to actually and physically put this realization into practice. Through this love for me as a child of His, God remains close by my side, every minute of every day. He is just as interested in helping me through moments of what can only be described as uncomfortable, as well as times of sheer desperation.

One long weekend, I was at work at the grocery store when we began to get particularly busy. I noticed that in the lineup of customers for my till, about third or fourth down, was a man who I felt betrayed by, and I only held hate and loathing for him. I was not pleased at all to see him, and certainly did not appreciate the fact that he was in the lineup for my till. I was the only cashier open, which meant that I would have no choice but to serve him. I could feel myself wavering between furious rage and extreme anxiety.

I checked my watch. My co-worker was only half way through her coffee break, and would not be back to open her till for at least eight minutes. There wasn't enough of a line up to warrant calling her away from her break to help me out. Everyone in line had only small orders. I had no excuse for not handling these customers by myself. The only real issue here was that I did not want to serve this man. I did not want to have to speak to him politely as I would be required to. I didn't even want to look at him. In fact, how dare he be here in my space? I was at work and I had to be here. He could go buy his armload of stuff somewhere else. My mind started freaking out with conflicting emotions running randomly rampant. Automatically, I served two customers, anxiously feeling that there was absolutely *no way* I could ever handle a civil transaction with this individual who was inching closer to my till. I had absolutely no way out of my dilemma. There was nowhere to go. I would surely end up getting fired from my job for what was sure to come out of my mouth when I did have to acknowledge his presence in front of me.

The only thing I could think of doing was to offer up a quick and panicked prayer (which some call an arrow prayer), "Help me, Jesus, to get through this".

Immediately, I heard a calm voice merely state a fact, *"He's uncomfortable too."*

Where did *that* come from? I was only concerned about how I was feeling and my end of the transaction. I really did not care in the least about how he was feeling. Why did God answer me this way? Was I supposed to care about him? Not likely!

"Uncomfortable" is putting it real mildly. I was quickly heading towards full-blown rage and panic. I was also surprised to hear an answer so quickly, immediately, within a fraction of a second actually, after my request for help.

Suddenly, my co-worker appeared at the next till, back unusually early from her break. She opened for business, and off he went to her till. Here was literally an answer to my prayers before my very eyes.

In the overall scheme of things, this was a very small issue, although it was an extremely emotional one for me. Immediately, within seconds of my 'arrow prayer', God provided a way!

God knew my heart. He was fully aware that in my heart I was harboring feelings of absolute hate and disgust for this person, and yet He still answered my prayer immediately. Not only that, when He did answer my prayer, it was within a fraction of a second.

I was surprised that a solution was found so quickly. Why should I feel surprised, though? He is God, after all. He is with me always, in my past and in my future. I had sent up an 'arrow prayer' because I have learned at Bible Study that is what Christians do, and then I was surprised that He actually found a way to immediately answer my prayer, because logically, I could not figure out a way out of the situation. In all honesty, though, I did not really appreciate the words that I had heard, nor the implication that I was supposed to care about how he was feeling. Maybe this one was going to take time on my part.

I obviously have a very long way to go in developing a faith that does not leave me surprised when He does what He promises in the Bible time and time again.

Psalm 5:1, 2
"O Lord, hear me as I pray; pay attention to my groaning. Listen to my cry for help, my King and my God, For I pray to no one but you."

Chapter 17

Thoughts Are Things

The years spent dealing with extreme family issues eventually began to affect my wellbeing. I felt exhausted and angry, and did not really know why or how to help myself out of the miserable state I was in.

One evening, as I passed by my husband in the hallway, I actually saw with my own eyes as I felt a strange blackness close in around me. It began with my peripheral vision and then moved inward until I was entirely encompassed by what appeared to be a massive black void. I was in this disturbing 'space' for what seemed to be at least seven to ten seconds. Here, I saw only black and, for the first time in my life, experienced absolute nothingness. There was a complete absence of any emotion or feeling whatsoever in the black void surrounding me. It was the emptiest, most hollow several seconds in my entire life.

I heard the voice again, *"There is no love here."*

I had been physically projected into the center of a black and all-consuming emotional void. This extreme experience of my living, spiritual self actually *being* in a black void and *feeling* absolutely nothing, no emotion what so ever, was extremely alarming. It was like experiencing being dead while still alive. It also made me realize the heartbreaking state in which my life was headed.

For the following three days, I felt extremely upset and unnerved by what I had just experienced. I was also made aware of the fact that I was being very unpleasant to live with, although I had conveniently justified my actions in my own mind. As I thought about it more, I became confused about what it actually meant.

Galatians 5:14, 15

"For the whole law can be summed up in this one command: "Love your neighbors as yourself." But if you are always biting and devouring one another, watch out. Beware of destroying one another."

I began to think that the words which had been spoken to me were to mean that perhaps I should consider a separation. After all, the Bible clearly warns against being 'unequally yoked', which means a Christian married to a non-Christian:

2 Corinthians 6:14, 15

"Don't team up with those who are unbelievers. How can righteousness be a partner with wickedness? How can light live with darkness? ...How can a believer be a partner with an unbeliever?"

By this point in time, I knew that I was definitely not going to revert back to living without God in my life, and my husband was certainly not going to become a Christian, so our home remained clearly divided. Perhaps a separation was the next logical step I needed to consider.

Just as I spent a few days thinking along the lines about how to begin taking my life in a different direction, I heard the precious voice again, *"My love is sufficient for you."*

What did that even mean? Am I where God wants me to be, or am I not?

I prayed for clarity.

It came in a set of three 'signs'. Immediately, that very same day, I received three small, separate gestures of affection from my husband. I had learned by now through Bible study that if something is mentioned or happens three times in the Bible, it is important. Here was my answer, given to me very clearly. Separation is definitely not the direction that God wanted me to go in.

With this decision made for me, I now knew that I needed to change my thinking, intentionally, one thought at a time. I needed to start thinking positively and counting my blessings, focusing on my husband's good qualities instead of what annoys me. This seemingly simple task turned out to be much more difficult than I imagined it would be.

I had to intentionally focus on positive thoughts as soon as I realized that I was in a negative headspace. It's not as if there were nothing positive to focus on, but rather it seemed that negative thoughts were able to pop into my mind rapidly and effortlessly, with extreme ease. Positive thoughts, on the other hand, were a different matter altogether. I practically had to physically, visually, and intentionally drag them into my mind through sheer will-power, and then work at having them stay there. It was much easier for me to be angry than to be positive.

I needed to accept the fact that my husband and I we were not on the same page, and perhaps never would be again, on the matter of God. I needed to make more of an effort to simply enjoy being with him again, regardless of that fact.

At this point in my life, I seemed to be having a hard time letting go of the idea that my life would be so much easier if we were "equally yoked". Every Sunday I watched married couples in church together and could not help but admire the fact that they were both in the same headspace, working together, with God at the center of their lives, towards a common goal.

I realized how dangerous it was for me to think along those lines. My admiration for Christian couples was not only making me unhappy in my personal situation, but it also broke the ninth commandment: "Thou shalt not covet...." Up until now, I had associated coveting only in reference to material possessions, but clearly it could be applied here, also.

In all fairness to my husband, we were "equally yoked" when we met, with neither of us being Christian. My husband is still in the place that we both were in when we fell in love with each other so many years ago, the place of living without God. It is me who has changed, and now we were not on the same page anymore.

Even though my husband never wants to discuss Christianity, he does support me in other ways. Whenever we travel, wherever we happen to be on a Sunday, he will help me to look for a church of my choice in that area. Then, he will wait around for the hour or so while the church service takes place, finding something else to do in the immediate area, wherever we happen to be, while I enjoy the luxury of attending a church service and getting spiritually recharged. Also, shortly after my father died, he bought me a beautiful gold chain with a crucifix pendant, knowing very well that I would cherish it forever, even though he did not believe in Christianity.

I realize that I need to sincerely pray for love to come back into my heart, and for joy to come back into my half of our marriage. I receive comfort from our Lord's promise to us in His Word, the precious Bible, that He will never leave me, nor forsake me.

My heavenly Father has lifted the veil from my eyes so that I can see the world around me differently, and include Him in my everyday life. God has also instilled in my heart a sincere love for Him. In my life, I have experienced life with God, and life without God, and I will never live without God again.

I need to trust that since it was God who changed me, He will stay with me and help me with my marriage. Because He loves my husband also, I have to leave the problem in His capable hands to work out the details in His timing.

John 14:15-17

"If you love me, obey my commandments. And I will ask the Father, and he will give you another Advocate, who will never leave you. He is the Holy Spirit, who leads into all truth. The world cannot receive him, because it isn't looking for him and doesn't recognize him. But you know him, because he lives with you now and later will be in you."

Chapter 18

Bible Study

It was March, 1997. I had spent the morning in Ladies Bible Study, totally immersed in God's word, surrounded by beautiful, fellow Christian ladies who had become my friends. I was beginning to thrive on this Bible study that was becoming so meaningful in my life.

Several years ago, when I began going to church, I was invited time and again to join the Ladies Bible study group. I always declined, because it did not really appeal to me at all. It sounded like just a bunch of women who gathered over coffee and cookies to read and talk about the Bible. There was nothing formal about it, no minister or anything, and I could not imagine what benefit it would hold for me to go and spend a couple of hours with them, drinking coffee and eating cookies. What could they possibly find to talk about for two hours straight? It seemed like a waste of time to me.

Looking back, I believe that I also may have had the impression that I physically needed to be in "God's house", inside of the church, in order for His teachings to actually sink into my brain and thought process. Maybe it was because of the not-so- positive experience of the meditation group that I used to go to, when we met at someone's house. Several of us would meet at a certain house, and there in the living room is where we innocently gathered to learn all about New Age 'stuff'. To my way of thinking at the time, at a house, they could teach you anything. But at a church, somehow I felt 'protected', certain that it would surely only be God's word that I heard. Not only that, I was already doing something 'Christian' once a week, by going to church on Sunday, and that should be enough.

One day at coffee time after a church service, the topic of conversation at the table where I was sitting got around to the next morning's Bible study, which several ladies would be attending.

One Christian lady, who I respected greatly, very casually said, "You know, if I had to make a choice and only be able to go to one thing, I don't know which one I would choose – church or Bible study."

I could not believe my ears!

I was shocked that she was saying this out loud in the coffee room, *right in the church*, right after we just came out from a service. I felt like sprinting as far away from her as possible, *immediately*, before that bolt of lightning came booming down out of the sky and struck her stone dead right in front of me for saying such a thing; and in church, yet! This was absolutely preposterous! This had to be blasphemy of some sort! I sat there barely believing that this nice, sweet lady who I knew and respected would be brazen enough to say such a thing in church!

What on earth did they do at these Bible studies, that made this normally nice and sane woman speak out like that? It was definitely wise for me to stay away from them on Monday mornings. It was bad enough that I was getting comfortable going to church.

I continued going only to church and getting acquainted with the overall process of Christianity. The one thing that I found hard, however, was that I was not familiar with some of the language that was repeatedly used. I kept hearing many words and phrases throughout the services, in the sermons, hymns, and in readings, that I had never used before in my life, so therefore I did not know what they meant; words like repent, spiritual gifts, faith, false teachers, creed, idolatry, worship, tribulation, false prophets, glorify and glorification, heresy, forsake, altar, anointed, atonement, consecrated, commandments, fellowship, foreordained, chalice, host, offering, ... the list went on and on. I may as well be learning a different language. Some of these words I had literally never even heard of before. At times, I felt that I was missing the main point of a sermon or a story because of my lack of understanding about one or more of these specific words that had been used that day. I did not feel comfortable asking anyone what these particular words meant, though, so I just learned what I could from what I did manage to understand.

On the up side, many of the stories that were read aloud seemed to revolve around stuff that I *was* familiar with. I grew up on a farm, so could easily relate to stories about goats, flocks of sheep and the importance of the shepherds who tended to them, bread, salt, and dealings with regular people and feelings about siblings, crops, fields that needed to be planted and harvested, seeds, good soil and bad soil, and rocky soil. Those simple words immediately transport me back to my childhood to one very specific field on my grandfather's farm which seemed to magically reproduce new

176

rocks every year that we picked mountains of. I also loved that each story had a point, some being clearer than others.

There finally came a point in time when I seemed to have a lot of questions about the stories in the Bible which were read to us on Sunday mornings. Maybe going to Bible Study on Monday mornings would not be such a bad idea, after all, since that was exactly what they did there – talk about and clarify the very same stories from that Bible. Not wanting to appear too eager or even particularly interested, I casually asked Betty who all attended these studies. She mentioned several names, and I was pleased that I recognized almost all of them. They were not just ladies who came to church, but several were people who I knew as customers from helping them at my place of work, or else casual acquaintances around town. Betty again reassured me that they were a very casual group, and that I was very welcome to just go once and try it. I said I might consider it. I still had my independent streak and pride to keep intact, so I could not appear too eager!

In the meantime, I was slowly developing a wonderful friendship with Betty. When her beloved husband, my Reverend Godfrey, passed away, she acquired a little dog, a perky little black and white terrier that she named Maggie Muggins. Muggins had lots of energy, so I offered to take her out for walks with me and my little dog whenever I went. Sometimes, if I did not want to walk, I would pick up Betty and Muggins, and we would get a coffee for each of us from the Petro Can station, then we would drive out into the back country. I would let the dogs out to run while we drove along very slowly; enjoying our coffee and our time together while the dogs got their exercise.

177

It was during these drives that I got to see how Betty was so easily able to relate the ancient stories from the Bible into relatable parables for everyday life today. She effortlessly wove together scenes and stories from the Biblical times together with the scenes and stories (often featuring problems or experiences that popped up in my life) from our own lives and the wilderness through which we drove. She had a remarkable gift of noticing the symbolism of what we talked about and what was visually around us in the forest that God had created. As I got to feel more comfortable listening to her speak very matter-of-factly about Biblical things, I also came to the conclusion that Bible Study at her house would be a good thing for me to try, at least once.

So, one Monday morning, I physically took my Bible in my hand, stepped out of my house with it, and intentionally walked down to Betty's house for Bible Study. I was surprised, however, to realize that I was entirely out of my comfort zone, yet again.

The whole time I was walking the very short distance, I was plagued with thoughts like: "What on earth am I doing now?", "My husband is going to be absolutely furious when he finds out that I'm doing this," and "What is wrong with me that I feel I have to go here?"

Thank goodness for the simple fact that I was going to my friend's house. That helped… alot! She had been graciously hosting Bible Studies at her house for years. I arrived with my Bible, and found a spot to sit at her kitchen table. Before long, there were about eight or nine of us gathered there. We chatted comfortably while sipping coffee and yes, enjoying fresh homemade cookies.

When the pleasantries were out of the way, and everyone was comfortably seated at the table, around 9:30 a.m., the conversation began to focus on health concerns of friends, family or neighbors of those of us gathered there. I assumed they were all just catching up on news from around town and within their families, and sharing this information with each other just for interest's sake. I, personally, thought it was a bit of a depressing topic to be discussing so early in the morning: who was sick and who was in the hospital, who needed surgery and who had a relative with problems, who was dealing with a death, etc. I had been expecting something a little more upbeat and happy. When it seemed as though there were no more health issues to discuss and the flow of conversation slowed down, I was secretly very happy to be done with this topic so that maybe we could finally get on with whatever they did to actually study the Bible.

Right then, we were all asked to bow our heads in prayer, and Betty said a prayer out loud. She began by thanking God for every single person gathered there, and naming off many blessings that she was thankful for. Then, much to my surprise, she began to individually name each person that had just been previously discussed in regards to their specific health concerns. Every individual name was tenderly lifted to God in prayer. When I thought we were just talking casually, sort of gossiping, while I was not so patiently waiting to actually get started, every friend, neighbor, and family member mentioned earlier was prayed for individually for his or her specific health or personal issue. It was done in the most loving and caring fashion that I had ever had had the opportunity to witness.

179

There was no gossiping or putting anyone down. There was no difference in attitude towards disagreeable and cranky people or pleasant, easy going ones. Each person was spoken of with total respect, regardless of their reputation. I never heard a single one of them speak with unkind words or an unkind tone of voice about anyone. The phrases that were so commonly used in my conversations with my other friends certainly had no place here.

I was more used to hearing and speaking phrases like:
"You should see what they did!"
"Do you know what she said?"
"It couldn't happen to a nicer guy."
"They're so miserable I want to run the other way when I see them coming."
"They got what they deserved."
"I go the other way whenever I see them coming."
"What goes around, comes around"
"What do they expect?"
"That's why nobody likes him (or her)."
"They're always complaining about being sick. Hypochondriacs."

With this particular bunch of women that were now sitting around me, just the problem itself was addressed, and lovingly given over to God in prayer, in seemingly total faith that He would take care of it.

Where were these people from, anyway, that they *all* thought and talked like that? I quickly decided that I'd better keep my mouth shut, because my way of speaking was certainly different from their way.

Next, a very short bit of the Bible was read, and then came the absolute very best part of all for me. Bible passages being discussed were explained in everyday language, sentence by sentence if need be, and people asked questions about what they did not understand, or else paraphrased it using different words but allowing the meaning to stay the same. This alone clarified things for me. Some mentioned an incident from their own lives that was similar, and how it worked out if they followed the example of how to deal with it in the Bible. Individual words were explained. Concepts were clarified. I felt as though I were in absolute heaven on earth! Finally I could actually understand and decipher some of the biblical words and phrases that were so totally foreign to me. Here *exactly* was the one thing we could not do in church during a service - ask questions and discuss what certain Bible passages meant.

I felt a peace in my soul that seemed to reach to the very core of my being. Finally, I would be able to actually understand the Bible. There was no doubt in my mind that I was doing the right thing by coming to Bible study! What a joyous revelation this was for me. I absolutely loved it! I was eager to go to Bible study regularly.

I rapidly learned that I knew absolutely nothing!

In fact, it was so bad that I sometimes felt embarrassed that I did not even know anything considered to be basic gospel truths that even the youngest of little children learn in Sunday school. So for the first several meetings, I rarely spoke, not trusting myself to say anything out loud. I felt it would be wiser and also safer for me to just listen to the conversation around the table, and learn that way.

The opportunity to listen to several people speak from their own perspective about one particular story from the Bible was opening up a whole new world for me. There seemed to be several correct ways to interpret the meanings and lessons learned from each story that presented itself. These ladies were all obviously old hats at these types of discussions, and were miles ahead of me in understanding the concepts presented in the Bible. While I was ecstatic about discovering the surface meaning about some stories, they were all diving deep into the moral implications of it.

For instance, like why a rainbow appeared after a rain. Up until now, I totally believed what my science teacher had taught us many years ago in regards to this issue. It had something to do with water particles that remained suspended in the atmosphere immediately after a rain, and when the sun shone upon them, it reflected to form a rainbow. Somehow, prisms were involved here, too, I think. This is an extremely simplified version, since science was never my strong suit and that all took place very long ago. Today that is all I remember on the topic of rainbows. However, my science teacher had a much longer explanation than that, backed up by pictures and long, scientific words which in the end made perfect sense to me, so therefore I held that as a truth.

The Bible, on the other hand, had a whole long, meaningful story, which included Noah, (of all things!), associated with the simple little fact of why a rainbow appears after a rain. I honestly thought that the story of Noah's Ark was merely a cute little fairy tale told to amuse children. As an adult, my entire knowledge of Noah's Ark came from my interpretation of the song by the Irish Rovers: Noah was just a make believe guy who built a make believe boat called an ark because God told him to. Then, when the rains came down, he loaded up the animals, two by two, and everyone got on except the unicorns, because they were playing in the rain. I don't know all the words to that song. I just liked the melody and the beat.

For starters, I was amazed that it was an event that was actually recorded in the Bible, in detail. Then, to learn that every single rainbow that appears after a rain is a specific sign from God to remind us that it is His promise to never flood the earth again... well, here was something with some substance to it! It gave me a whole new sense of wonderment to ponder upon whenever I did look at a rainbow.

Suddenly, the fact of *how* a rainbow appears was not nearly as important as *why* a rainbow appears. Bible study was encouraging me to think about things on a deeper level. Up until now, when I marveled at the beauty and phenomena of a rainbow, I would think of light reflecting off water molecules in the air, creating the beautiful image before me. From now on, after this Bible Study lesson, when I marveled at the phenomena of a rainbow, I would know that God was right there, lovingly showing it to me and everyone else nearby to see it as a reminder to us of His promise in His Word in the Bible that He will never flood the earth again.

Many other songs, too, that I was familiar with, seemed to have some sort of connection with the Bible.

> "Run, Sampson, run, Delilah's on her way
>
> Run, Sampson, run, you ain't got time to stay…"

Who would have thought that Sampson and Delilah were actual, real people who once lived, and were mentioned in the Bible, of all places? My love for music proved to be somewhat helpful in the fact that I knew at least some words to some country and western songs whose lyrics mentioned people in Biblical passages. As these were newly discovered by me and discussed within the group, I could relate to at least somewhat to words in songs I had heard. At the very least, I knew that Sampson was very strong, and he lost all his strength when Delilah, 'the gal with the cheating heart' tricked him and cut his hair off and he lost all his strength.

Good grief. What a thing to base a scrap of intellect on!

I rapidly grew to feel very close to these ladies. What was spoken there was not to be repeated outside the group, because many discussions led to personal accounts of private matters that one only discusses with best and trusted friends. Within the Bible study group, I noticed that the answers to personal concerns that someone was struggling with at the time always came from the Bible. No matter what sort of problem arose; there was always a parallel story in the Bible, with a wise and loving solution available… always.

It was exactly what my new Christian coworker and friend had told me long ago, "The answers to everything you need to know are in the Bible. You just have to look for it." This fact was popping up again in my life.

Special prayers were always said for people facing difficult situations. The prayers always included asking for wisdom in the decisions that needed to be made. Here was another concept totally foreign to me. These people actually *asked* God to give them wisdom regarding a troubling situation, and fully expected that God would not only hear their prayer but also answer it.

When prayers were answered, usually several weeks or months later, these were also discussed again, but this time with thanksgiving. God always got the glory, absolutely always. Not the members in the group, or the leader of the group. It was always God. This was surely different that the way of thinking that I had as a non-Christian.

I was more familiar in the world of:
"You have to look after yourself. No one else will."
"Take what is rightfully yours."
"Don't get mad, get even."
"Look out for Number One."
"I must have been a ...(something or other) in my previous life because this is happening to me now."
"Shoot for the top, command respect."
"An eye for an eye."
"The squeaky wheel gets the grease."
"Me first."

"You scratch my back and I'll scratch yours."

In my regular world, also, if a person gave you good advice, they were the ones who got recognition for wise advice, and all recognition and praise went to them specifically, along with a certain amount of earned respect. Here at Bible study, we were being encouraged to give all the praise for all wise counsel to God and His Word in the Bible.

I already felt inadequate at Bible study, no matter how nice everyone was. I sincerely felt that if I ever did manage to come up with something 'wise' to say that actually helped someone, then I too would surely have to pass any praise for 'my' words on towards God also, since everybody else was doing it. If things went this way, I would surely have no self-esteem left whatsoever by the time I was done here. After all, if I were talking to my regular friends and actually came up with a good idea that helped them to solve a problem in their life, or at least shed light on it, I would at least get *some* credit for it. These ladies were saying that the credit should all go to God, because all wisdom comes from God. How would I ever feel good about myself if I was going to have to start thinking like this?

Even though there were some differences in what I was learning here, many things that my mother and father and grandparents had taught me while I was growing up were confirmed to be absolutely true. They were just worded differently.

My father had a colorful way with words: "Don't think you're better than anybody else!" or, more to the point - "Who the hell do you think you are?"

186

The Bible's wording was, "God created all man equal".

I used to think that it was our family's way of looking at things, or perhaps the Doukhobor way to treat all others with respect, but apparently it was also God's way. There were many such similarities, words phrased differently to mean the same thing.

At one Bible study, it was pointed out that each and every Christian worldwide prayed the words, "Our Father" to begin the Lord's Prayer as taught to us by Jesus. Individually, then, this meant that if He is my father, and He is your father, that makes us *all* His children. Therefore, we are all sisters and brothers in Christ. Best of all, God was our Heavenly Father that we could speak to every day, at any time.

Later on, as we further studied the Lord's Prayer, we came to the phrase, "Forgive us our trespasses as we forgive those who trespass against us..." The first four words were direct, we were asking God to forgive us for any wrongdoings we may have intentionally or unintentionally done against Him or someone else in our everyday speaking and actions. For instance, the times when I felt a twinge of guilt, regret or sorrow about something I had said or done, this twinge was from God. It was His way of letting me know that what I did was wrong, and I needed to go to Him in prayer, and ask Him for His forgiveness. By doing so, I was not only admitting my wrong and therefore being accountable for it, but I was also raising my own awareness of tiny ways in which I needed to change so that I would be living (conducting my words and actions) in a manner more pleasing to my Heavenly Father. This would ultimately lead to peace in my soul, the very peace which had eluded me for years, *and the* very coveted "peace that passes all understanding" that was spoken of in the Bible and in church.

I felt absolutely euphoric. Why was not every single person in the world sitting around a kitchen table getting refreshed and rejuvenated by God's Word?

Bible Study continued and we began to focus on the last six words, "forgive those who trespass against us..."

Whoa!!! Really?

I did not like where this was going, not even a little bit. There were some people that I didn't mind being furious with and holding grudges against. These people deserved it if I was angry at them. My anger gave me a sense of power and control in this situation. I could not look at them as brothers and sisters. I felt annoyed just thinking of them. They had wronged me and I felt offended. I had been fuming at some of them for years. No way was I just going to forgive them and pretend that everything was okay, Bible Study or no Bible Study!

Not going to happen! Period!

God was able to forgive me because He was God. I was just a human. I had feelings that had been hurt. I was not capable of being big enough to forgive the really hurtful stuff, and besides, why should I?

I continued looking for excuses for hanging onto my rebellious thoughts, but the more we studied God's Word, the clearer it became to me that I was hurting only myself by not forgiving others. For my own sake, then, it would be wise for me to actually learn *how* to forgive someone I had been angry at for years. Thankfully, I was in the right place for that. The Bible was full of stories, phrases, and gems of wisdom that seemed to literally pop up and grab my attention just when I needed to hear them most. It never ceased to amaze me that whenever something was weighing very heavily on my mind, an answer or a solution would literally appear out of nowhere, exactly when I needed it.

Ephesians 1: 16, 17

"I have not stopped thanking God for you. I pray for you constantly, asking God, the glorious Father of our Lord Jesus Christ, to give you spiritual wisdom and insight, so that you might grow in your knowledge of God."

Chapter 19

The Vision of the Little Tree

Most of the ladies at Bible study had much more "experience" with Christianity than I did. Almost all the group had grown up in Christian homes, and had family members that were active Christians in their communities. Some were even professionals, working as missionaries or ministers. All of the ladies were familiar with Sunday school, having attended it when they were young. Several ladies had also been Sunday school teachers. This was all very different from my upbringing. I had done my best going through life with a very different mindset.

One morning the discussion led to the topic of how different people tend to deal with problems during times of difficulty. The common consensus around the table in times of crisis seemed to be turning to God and Jesus in prayer immediately, asking for help from the heavenly realm. I was thirty six years old when I had the vision of Jesus, and up until then, I wasn't even aware that there was a God who loved me and who was willing to help me with every single problem that came my way. I simply made the best decision possible with the knowledge that I had. Most times I would discuss the circumstances with people around me, and base my decisions on what felt right when I considered all the advice. I did not know even know that prayer to a living God, my very Creator, was an option. I just automatically figured that I had to do everything by myself in the best way I knew how. Turmoil, emotional upheaval, indecision, sleepless nights, and restlessness generally accompanied me during times of trouble.

As the discussion at the Bible study proceeded, *every single lady present* made a comment like, "I can't understand how anyone would not know to turn to Jesus during times of difficulty," or "I have always known that Jesus is there for me". Someone else said, "Ever since I can remember, I have been hearing stories from the scriptures."

It's like they were from another planet!

Slowly, it began to dawn on me. They would never be able to really understand me. It was not their fault; we were merely much too different! They were comfortable here. This *was* their way of life, and the only life that they knew. It was me that did not fit in here. I was the one trying to fit in where I did not belong. These ladies would never have to change. They were born into this lifestyle and belief system. They belonged here. It was me that did not.

Suddenly, I very much felt like a fish out of water. I had only recently figured out and barely understood who the Holy Spirit was; let alone how to let Him help me. As much as I was learning and enjoying the company of these ladies, I suddenly realized that there was too big of a gap in our lives. How could I ever expect them to understand where I was coming from, when this had been their life all along? It was me who was out of

191

place here, not them. I really did not know anything at all, and it was especially embarrassing that I did not even know any of the 'basics'. I felt like a kindergartener thrown into a Grade Six class and expected to understand and keep up at that level. I still didn't even understand the meanings of many commonly used words in the Bible, and for every word I did learn the meaning of, there seemed to be ten new ones that I did not have a clue as to what they meant. Sometimes I would ask for a word to be explained, but if I didn't immediately understand the explanation, I felt guilty because of the time that was being wasted describing it to me, while everyone else was discussing issues at a much more intellectual level. I felt like I was holding up the whole class from progressing at a pace that they were all used to keeping before I joined the group.

When this particular Bible study was over, I left feeling extremely out of sorts, almost to the point of being miserable. I went for a long walk in the woods to try and clear my head and to figure out where I was at in my life. It was an overcast day, and the dreary clouds mirrored my mood. The dogs (mine and Betty's), were always a pleasure to take into the forest. They ran around excitedly, exploring the many curious scents that their sensitive noses detected. Whenever I whistled, they would come bounding towards me with great enthusiasm. I hoped that some of their zeal would rub off on me and bring me out of the slump I was in.

As I walked amongst the trees listening to the occasional bird singing or a squirrel chattering, I felt very close to God, as I often do while walking peacefully in His world. Here, in this forest, basically untouched by human hands except for the occasional dirt road, everything was exactly as it should be. Here, life was simple and perfect. The trees and the grass grew and died in their due seasons, each plant and tree attracted a specific bird or animal for food or shelter, fresh water flowed down a little creek bed as it had for probably hundreds of years. This is where I needed to be to find peace with God, not trying to force myself to fit in at a place where I did not belong.

I reflected upon the morning's Bible study, sorting out in my mind the main objectives of the teachings and how they applied to me in my life right now. I also thought about the conversation between the ladies, their comments, and particularly how they did not understand someone not turning to Jesus Christ in times of trouble. I tried to visualize what their lives would have been like, growing up in homes where God's word was used freely in everyday life. I realized that I could no more imagine this than they could imagine growing up without God in their lives, as I had. As this realization became clearer to me, I understood why they could not relate to non-Christians in some ways. They had never known any other way of life, other than one in which there was a strong familiarity with God, Jesus Christ, and the Holy Spirit.

Suddenly I felt even more inadequate about being in their company, trying to learn about and fit into 'their' world. We may as well be from different planets. They would never understand me and I would never understand them.

I was going to have to quit going to Bible Study. I clearly did not belong there. This decision felt totally right. I would not go back again. My mind was made up!

Immediately, a wave of utter exhaustion swept over me very suddenly and strongly. I felt extremely weak in the knees... too weak to continue walking. There was a large rock only a few steps away, so I walked over to it and sat down, resting my elbows on my knees and putting my forehead into the palms of my hands. I felt totally exhausted and deflated. I do not know how long I sat like that, perhaps two minutes or maybe three.

When I wearily looked up, a most spectacular sight awaited me.

My eyes were seeing a Holy vision!

In the vision, the formation of the trees at that exact spot in front of me was such that there were several full grown, tall, strong, and older trees forming a sort of semi-circle in a wee, grassy clearing. In the center of that semi-circle was a new little tree, seemingly carefully sheltered in their midst. At that exact moment, a ray of sunshine broke through the dark, cloudy sky, sending a brilliant stream of light upon the tiny tree in the middle.

Suddenly, the meaning of the vision became crystal clear to me. My very own spiritual life was being represented in the vision by that little tree in the forest clearing. At Bible study, I *was* the new growth, just like the tiny tree was the new growth in the middle of the forest. While at Bible study, I was surrounded by spiritually older Christians, solid and strong in their faith. In God's forest, the tiny tree was sheltered from storms by the stable, sturdy, and magnificent pines growing closely together around it. At Bible study, I was spiritually sheltered, encouraged, and guided through life's storms by my Christian sisters, just as the little tree was sheltered and protected from storms by the taller, older trees in a perfect semi-circle around it.

My spirit was immediately rejuvenated by the vision.

I did belong at Bible Study after all! I wanted to be there, I needed to be there, and the vision confirmed that I did belong there, after all. Relief flooded through me. I would keep going to Bible study and learning more of God's Word, as I had been previously doing.

I stood up from the rock, and continued on with my walk through forest with a joyously uplifted heart. Since that day, I have walked that same path many times. Although the trees in that exact spot are in a vague, semi-circle shape, and there is, indeed, one smaller, younger tree in the middle of the circle, they have never again looked as crystal clear as they did during the vision. I do, however, fondly remember the vision that God freely showed me at that very spot and I always feel especially close to God while I am there. (Incidentally, this scene is the painting on the cover of this book.)

Later on, I privately shared this vision with Betty. I did not particularly want to share something personal like this vision with more than maybe one or two people, extremely close friends, and only on a one to one basis when I felt the time was right and it was safe to do so. I was rather fond of my privacy, and I felt that this was a rather personal revelation meant for only me.

Although I was rejuvenated about going to Bible Study, I was still very quiet while I was there, not wanting to draw attention to my apparent lack of knowledge any more than what was already painfully obvious. I was not comfortable speaking out in this little group, no matter how nice they all were. After all, all these ladies were old hands at Christianity. They were just as comfortable going to Bible study and church as I was going to the post office to check my mail. I do not know what it is like to have been a Christian all of one's life, but I did feel rather sure that I was in a place far behind where they were at in our learning, and therefore I really had nothing to offer them. I considered telling them about the vision, but decided that at the most, they would perhaps find it mildly interesting, but it would really be of no value to them.

Betty, however, had other ideas. When I had initially told her about the vision, she suggested that I share it with the group. I told her that I was not comfortable with that idea, but I would think about it.

The very next Monday during Bible Study, during a little lull in the morning's conversation, she enthusiastically announced, "Thelma shared something with me the other day that she would very much like to share with you!"

Apparently I was taking too long to think about it!

Immediately, I felt my stomach tighten up in a knot. This sweet little lady just booted me right out of my comfort zone without even flinching. She knew exactly what she was doing, too. My normally warm, fuzzy feelings towards her cooled off slightly as I briefly experienced a feeling that I had just been tricked! I had no choice now but to speak, since everyone was sitting there looking at me expectantly. I hadn't rehearsed anything, so I just quietly and slowly related the steps of what happened exactly one week prior. Much to my surprise, they *were* sincerely interested. They even seemed enthusiastically encouraged by what had taken place after our last Bible Study together.

I was slowly beginning to realize how important it is to share our experiences, especially positive and uplifting ones. I had been under the impression that once a person became a well-grounded Christian that was that. You were 'there', and did not necessarily need any more day-to-day encouragement. Sure, I, personally, benefited so much from listening to others tell of their experiences, but I was new at this.

I also realized that my beautiful friend and Bible study leader was gently nudging me out of my comfort zone, encouraging me to actually participate in the Bible study. It was for my own good, I see that now. Not that she gave me any choice.

Apparently I needed to learn and also believe that I have something worthwhile to offer to the group, also. It is through sharing and talking that we encourage one another to stay on the Christian path, so we can all enjoy God's grace. Interesting!

Philippians 4: 8, 9
"And now, dear brothers and sisters, one final thing. Fix your thoughts on what is true, and honorable, and right, and pure, and lovely, and

admirable. Think about things that are excellent and worthy of praise. Keep putting into practice all you learned and received from me – everything you heard from me and saw me doing. Then the God of peace will be with you."

Chapter 20

Sharing God's Word

Little by little, I began to speak occasionally about Christian aspects that related to my everyday life and world around me with people other than the ladies in my Bible study group. At first, I did so mostly with my daughters, because they were a very safe starting point for me. They seemed to tolerate my new way of thinking without giving me any negative feedback, so I began to feel confident that by very carefully voicing tiny bits of this new way of thinking, I must be on the right track.

Eventually I began to dare to insert Christian facts into conversations with my closest friends, if it felt right to do so at the time. It would only be perhaps a sentence or two here and there, in a safe place with individuals whom I felt would not be offended by what I had to say, nor be confrontational to me because what I was thinking and saying was different from the normal way in which we usually shared conversations. When I recognized and felt that something I had learned from the scriptures could be applied to the present conversation, and I felt definitely clear about it, and if I also felt brave, I would state my new take on the situation, out loud.

For example, once a friend and I were chatting nonchalantly about our jobs. This conversation eventually led to each of us complaining about the fact that we did not particularly enjoy having to get up early in the mornings to go to work. These complaints would go on and on, back and forth, until each of us had sufficiently vented our woes.

Eventually, my friend said, "In my next life, I'm going to come back as some rich old lady's pampered poodle!"

Normally, we would have a good chuckle and then I would agree that that was a terrific idea. This time, however, I chose to speak out.

I casually said, "That would be good except that there is no such thing as a 'next life'. We are only here on earth one time. It says that in the Bible."

Then I would rapidly go into an inner panic, hoping that no confrontation was coming at me about this new little 'fact' that I had dared to insert into our friendly conversation. I did not yet feel confident enough to verbally have to defend my new way of looking at things.

What I surprisingly discovered, however, was that the more I spoke the words out loud, the more I began to really believe them in my heart, and therefore accept them as my truth. I felt absolutely marvelous to realize that I had my feet planted firmly on the ground about something as simple as this.

I remained very sensitive about not 'preaching' the Scriptures to other people; so many times I had to contain the enthusiasm that I felt about freely sharing God's Word. I did not want to put anyone off by 'being pushy' just because something was new and important and exciting to me.

I also learned that I was not always going to merely be the recipient of God's Word. There came a point in time when God again nudged me out of my comfort zone, and actually gave me a very clear and specific opportunity to be the catalyst to share His word with someone else.

We had made plans one weekend to entertain company in our home.

The day before their arrival, I experienced what started out as a dream, and then a voice distinctly said, *"Tell him, 'God created all man equal.'"*

I woke up mortified! "Tell him?" Out loud?

Well, obviously it had to be done out loud. The voice did not say to write him a little note and pass it to him discreetly, then run away, which is really what I would much prefer to do, if I *had* to do anything at all. There was also no doubt in my mind as to whom I was to speak to. It was conveyed perfectly clearly that it was the gentleman half of our company we were expecting.

This could only mean one thing. I would have to intentionally initiate a conversation about God and Christianity and the Bible, and specifically pass this simple, five word message on to someone who was going to be a guest in our home. This was way out of my comfort zone, and I was not at all pleased by this request. But at the same time, how could I even entertain the idea of saying "no?"

The last thing I wanted to do is to 'preach' to him, giving him a message from God. I was totally uncomfortable with the idea of passing on that message. Whatever would my guest think of me if I did that? What was I supposed to say as to where the message came from? I would look like a total nut, and he would probably feel like avoiding me like the plague if this was the new direction in which our relationship was going to go. I couldn't just go around telling people that God spoke to me and this is what He said, and this message is for you!

He might also possibly think that I was meddling in his life, or worse yet, judging him, thinking that I was better than him, and I surely did not want to give him that impression of me. I felt that we had a good, friendly relationship, and I wanted to keep it that way. You know, not make any 'waves'. If I passed on that message, I could foresee all sorts of weird problems and insinuations happening. If I passed on that message, I would have to be extremely careful as to how I approached doing so.

Man oh man, this is not a place I ever expected to be in, nor was I happy in the least about being in.

Exodus 4:1
"But Moses protested again, "What if they won't believe me or listen to me? What if they say, 'The Lord never appeared to you?'"

I reprimanded myself sharply! I could not think along these lines. The first thing I had to do was change my thinking, because I had rapidly worked myself up into a state of anxiety and fretting!

First off, I had to change my thinking from '*if* I passed on the message' to '*when* I passed on the message,' no matter how scary that was. There is no way that I could not do what God asked of me. I could not bear to live with myself if I chickened out. I knew I would have to do it. I just didn't want to... not even a little bit. Never did I dream that I would ever be acting as a 'messenger' for Him, and definitely not so soon in my Christian walk. Maybe they would not be able to come, and we would have to cancel our visit.

No such luck. They arrived on schedule. When they came into our home, I greeted them warmly and pretended that I was happy to see them, which I was... sort of. However, I felt totally apprehensive about the evening ahead and the job that I knew I had to do. It remained in the back of my mind throughout the entire visit. Before I knew it, time was chugging along, and an opportunity had not yet presented itself so that I could give him the message in private, without anyone else around. I knew that I *had to* pass on the message, today, and I was, by now, at a point where I just wanted to get it over with so that I could relax and enjoy everyone's company.

So, while everyone was still all together visiting, with my task ahead weighing heavily on my mind, I took it upon myself to say that before they left, he and I had to go for a quick little drive because I needed to talk to him privately for just a moment.

Everyone gave me a rather surprised look at this unexpected announcement.

We did go for a short drive, and I told this fine gentleman what I had to say. It seemed to be received well, and I was extremely relieved that I had done what I needed to do. That was that!

Phew! What a load off my mind. This being a Christian is certainly not for sissies, that is for sure.

During the remainder of the visit, before they left for home, there came one small period of time when only he and I were in the living room together for several minutes. During this lull, it was strongly impressed upon me that this would have been the time to tell him privately, without bringing any attention what so ever to anyone else.

This was the point at which I learned one very important lesson. I needed to learn to trust God completely. If He gives me a specific job to do, He will also provide the absolute perfect and specific time for carrying it out, and also bring it to my attention that this is the correct time. I needed to learn and trust that He will also make me aware of this, His perfect timing, so that His work can be done here on earth. I also had to trust that He helped this gentleman hear what was being told to him with the words that I chose to use, or perhaps the words that God had given me for the task, at the time that I spoke to him, even though it was not in His perfect timing. I could only hope that I had not messed it all up by taking the matter of timing into my own hands.

Not only that, none of this was about me. This time, I am merely His messenger. A lot of my uncomfortable feelings about carrying out this specific task were derived from my "what will he think of me if I do what God asks?" head space. Also, I was concerned about what the others would think of me. In reality, this was really not about me at all. I was merely asked to pass on a specific message to someone else at His request. That is all. Then I need to leave that person in God's care, trusting that God knows what He is doing and why He is doing it.

I mostly need God's help to always keep these things in perspective.

Romans 10:14,15

"But how can they call on Him to save them unless they believe in Him? And how can they believe in Him if they have never heard about Him? And how can they hear about Him unless someone tells them? And how will anyone go and tell them without being sent? That is why the Scriptures say, 'How beautiful are the feet of messengers who bring good news.' "

Chapter 21

Voices and Visions of Guidance

As the months turned into years, different situations arose in which I was extremely blessed to hear the loving voice of my Heavenly Father help me to stay focused on the path that He was encouraging me to walk.

I was learning that there are many layers, so to speak, to prayers. The 'outer' layer was the obvious one. I would see and recognize a need or a problem, and verbally bring it before God. Sometimes, just the first step of verbalizing aloud helped me to see more clearly what exactly was bothering me in regards to particular emotional issues. Another layer, or aspect, of praying effectively was to be able to come to the place of trusting that prayer is a tangible 'thing'. Once the prayer was clarified in my mind and then spoken out loud to God, my job was to then let go and trust that God would look after whatever I had was released to Him in prayer. For me, this proved to be much easier said than done.

Once, in a personal situation involving an issue of trust with one of my fellow church members, I was beginning to harbor negative feelings towards this particular individual. When I discussed the problem in confidence with my friend and pastor, I was told that our job as Christians was to give it to God in prayer, and then let go of it. That seemed easy enough to do, so I did exactly that. I did pray and give it to God, but in no time at all, it was back on my mind again, and continuing to upset me. It seemed that no sooner did I release the problem to God in prayer, than I picked it right back up again. This happened over and over again, as I seemed to be unable to truly relinquish it to God in prayer. After all, I was used to figuring out and fixing things by myself. Perhaps I felt that since I could not see or figure out a solution to the problem, I could not possibly see how God was going to be able to fix it, either. Whatever my underlying reason was, apparently I had trouble letting it go and leaving it in God's capable hands.

One Sunday morning while I was sitting in church, waiting for the service to begin, this particular issue popped into my head, and again, I could feel myself sliding into a negative headspace because of it. I was not pleased that it was once more on my mind.

Suddenly, God's gentle voice spoke softly to me, *"Why are you so concerned about that?"*

It was absolutely true. Why, indeed, was I so concerned about that? Why did I keep hanging onto that negative train of thought after giving it to God? I had given it to Him many times already, He was aware of it, and therefore He would deal with the situation in the way that He knew was best, and in His time. Sitting there in church, it was strongly impressed upon me that I needed to look at that individual differently, and see them and recognize them as a child of God, just like me. We both had our faults, and we were both equally loved by our Heavenly Father. I had to trust that God knew what He was doing, and it was neither my place to meddle in, nor try to fix something after giving it to God to deal with. We are all in different places of learning, moving forward, and living as best as we can, and this individual was no different. Why would I expect more of them? Very shortly thereafter, this ceased to occupy my mind.

Matthew 7: 1, 3-5

"Do not judge others, and you will not be judged... And why worry about a speck in your friend's eye when you have a log in your own? How can you think of saying to your friend, 'Let me help you get rid of that speck in your eye' when you can't see past the log in your own eye? Hypocrite! First get rid of the log in your own eye; then you will see well enough to deal with the speck in your friend's eye."

* * *

At another time, the Lord's voice dealt directly with my health. Migraine headaches have run in our family for many generations. I remember my mother suffering with them for as long as I can recall. She, in turn, remembers her grandmother lying in bed in a darkened room for days, also suffering from migraine headaches. Her grandfather would go to town and buy pills for relief from the headaches. In those days, the specific pills that were used for treating migraine headaches were packaged with a few tablets inside a little paper packet. Several of these packets were stapled onto a long strip of cardboard, for individual sale at the general store. Grandfather Barisoff, however, would buy the whole strip. I suppose this was so that they were always able to have some on hand. My mother remembers, as a little girl, being fascinated with this long strip with the packets attached to it. I inherited migraine headaches, and have had them all my life. Both of my daughters also suffer terribly with them.

Several years ago, I was really sick in bed with an excruciating headache that just would not go away. It had the severity of an extremely bad migraine, which unfortunately, I frequently experience, yet this time, it somehow strangely different, although no less crippling. I was literally in bed for 4 days, with my stomach very upset, barely able to eat or drink anything. Then, suddenly, on the 5th morning I woke up feeling clearheaded and pain free. I lay in bed assessing what seemed to be a marvelous change in my health for the first time in days.

A voice came to me immediately: *"See how good you feel when you don't drink coffee!"*

Coffee???

I did feel much better, though, strangely like I was clean from the inside out. What could coffee possibly have to do with this? Not once did I ever associate my migraine headaches with my coffee consumption. Everyone in my family drinks coffee, and always has. Not to any extreme, just regular enjoyment of a couple of cups of coffee in the morning and occasionally a cup or two in the afternoon. If anything, when I did take migraine medication, I usually washed it down with a cup of coffee, believing that the caffeine in the coffee would help the medication to work faster and more effectively.

Although I seemed to be feeling fine for the first time in days, I certainly was none too pleased to hear those specific words. I greatly appreciated the fact that at least now I knew what was causing some of my headaches, but coffee, to me, was more than just a drink to consume. It was a very sociable activity, one that I enjoyed thoroughly with my husband, friends, and all of my family. I loved to go out for coffee, have friends in for coffee, and most of all, to enjoy a cup of the delicious brew while sitting outside in the fresh air, on the boat, in the early mornings with my husband when we were fishing and camping. It was part of my everyday life.

Within minutes of getting out of bed feeling great, I could already tell that this was going to be a tough habit to break. The very first thing I wanted to do, right then and there, was to brew up a fresh cup, sit down and enjoy both the scent and the flavor that I had come to associate with many pleasant times. It would be a kind of mini 'celebration' because my headache was gone.

I am embarrassed to admit that here it is, years later, and I am still struggling with having to cut coffee out of my diet completely. I still love the smell and taste. I have, however, stopped drinking it daily and cut back to enjoying an occasional cup or two perhaps once or twice a week. If I consume more than that, I not only suffer from headaches, but also a very upset stomach while feeling extremely irritable. I truly savor what little I do drink, but I really should cut it out totally. I do feel better if I don't touch it at all.

The flesh is so very weak!

* * *

I am not sure exactly what was going on in my life, nor the exact date when these next words were spoken to me.

I just know that I heard them loud and clear: *"Now is the right time."*

I found this to be an unusual and vague message to receive. I thoroughly assessed all aspects of my life at the time, and tried to figure out what God could possibly be referring to. Try as I might, I could not specifically put my finger on any one thing that it was the 'right time' to change or to address. We were not going to be making any major decisions, and there was no obviously stressful situation or crisis. This was one time that I should have heeded my mother's and father's wise words about paying attention to what was going on around me. I should have, at the very least, written down when those words were spoken to me. At least then I would have been able to look back to that point in my life and maybe see what was about to change.

In retrospect, I realized that some changes happen almost immediately while others come about very gradually. This must have been a gradual one, because I honestly cannot specifically and confidently pin point one particular aspect of my life that God's word was referring to.

As I record this, however, I feel that perhaps I may have heard these words at about the time that I began to have little nagging feelings that I should, in fact, become a bit more open about my own life. It took me a long time, several months or more, of going to Bible study once a week with the same group of ladies before I felt comfortable enough to open up and share anything personal with them, even though they all spoke openly about their own lives with me and with each other.

By sitting back and observing the honest and respectful communication between these beautiful ladies, I could clearly see the advantage of several people working together towards a common goal. There, together as a group, different methods of approaching a problem would be openly discussed without any fear or judgment whatsoever that someone else might think their idea was weird or foolish. I admired them greatly for openly sharing personal thoughts and feelings in this safe environment.

Even though I have always worked with the public and am comfortably outgoing, I have always been protective of my privacy when it came to my personal life. Other than family members and a few very close friends, I usually kept my interactions with others on a very surface level. Through

Bible study, however, I was learning how beneficial it was to sincerely listen to others and to openly share my own feelings with them. So many times, someone would bring up an issue that was bothering them, or perhaps they were unsure of as to how to deal with. Someone else in the group would more often than not refer to a similar incident from their personal experiences, or mention a related story from the Bible. Always, through honest discussion, a Biblical scripture would be found that was appropriate and provided clarity to the situation. Perhaps there was someone out there, too, who could somehow benefit from my speaking about my own life. I really could not imagine how, though. It seemed like my life was a mess more often than not, and I did not really know anything about Christianity.

Isaiah 30:21
"And your ears will hear a word behind you, this is the way, walk in it, whenever you turn to the right or to the left."

* * *

One day we went to visit friends who are very dear to my heart. I had heard rumblings that they were dealing with a problem of meddling from a strongly opinionated outsider who was aggressively criticizing one of them on a regular basis.

After the initial pleasantries were over, we walked into the kitchen and sat down at their table to visit over a cup of coffee. I was feeling very pleased and content to be in their presence and able to spend some very precious time with them. I comfortably and peacefully gazed around at the faces of those of us gathered around the table. When I looked at the person whom I had heard was under constant attack, their image was immediately shielded from my eyes.

In its place was a vision.

What I had seen with my eyes at that exact moment was a very large and extremely dark greyish brown area. In the center there was light, and within that light was a vision of a mouse backed into a corner.

It was impressed upon me this individual ('the mouse') was feeling trapped in a corner, and very aware of a great danger lurking in the darkness surrounding it. There was no feeling of fear associated with the vision, but rather one of mere fact. The vision stayed in front of me for several seconds, perhaps five to seven, before fading away.

Aware that I was back in reality and sitting amongst friends, I rapidly looked around the faces at the table to see if anyone had noticed that I had 'spaced out' for a few seconds. No one so much as even looked at me. I took it to mean that God was confirming to me that this person whom I cared about very much was under great attack right now. I needed to be sensitive and encouraging to them, and keep them at the forefront of my prayers.

Daniel 10: 7

"Only I, Daniel, saw this vision. The men with me saw nothing, but they were suddenly terrified and ran away to hide."

* * *

Since my father passed away at the young age of 56, my husband had suggested several times that my mother come on holidays with us. The three of us have always had lots of fun together. One such time, a situation arose at the beginning of a holiday where we three would be driving a great distance together for about two or three weeks. On this particular trip, my husband was strongly affected by events that had happened to him which he had no control over. As a result, one particular day when the problem must have been bothering him more than usual, he complained while we travelled in the privacy of our truck, and vented to me again after we went to bed.

As I lay there in the night thinking about what had been said, I felt myself growing increasingly irritated about the day's conversation. We were just starting out on this holiday, and I did not want to spend my time listening to negative talk about a situation that was beyond our control. As it often happens during the night, the situation began to get blown out of proportion in my mind the longer I dwelled on it. I began to feel apprehensive about having to travel many hours each day in the close confines of the cab of our truck in a negative atmosphere. Furthermore, I

215

was embarrassed that my husband was speaking in this manner in front my mother. The longer I lay in bed stewing, the more upset I got. All I wanted to do was enjoy our travelling time together, explore new places, and have a good time.

Some holiday this was going to be! I was sorry that I was even here! The angrier I became, the worse the situation looked. I lay awake in bed entertaining some very mean ideas of how to even up the score. I lay there for what seemed a long time, letting my anger fester. I dreaded the upcoming days, imagining the worst, and became furious at him because now it was his fault that I was upset and could not fall asleep. Worst of all, there was no way out of the situation as we were very far from home.

Just when I felt like there was no hope whatsoever for a pleasant holiday, I heard a loving voice speak words of encouragement to me, *"Lo, if I am with you, whom shall you fear?"*

That was a very realistic fact.

What was I actually fretting about, anyway? I had managed to work myself up into a state of turmoil just because someone close to me was upset.

I *know* better!

I didn't even make an attempt to pray about this. I just jumped straight into worry and anger. Instead of being infuriated or worrying about the negative headspace of someone else (which I have absolutely no control

216

over), and letting that snowball how I am going to deal with that in the upcoming days, I have the choice of actually doing something positive instead. I can intentionally focus my own thoughts and words on more positive things, and give this problem to God in prayer. After all, I know that God is with me all of the time, and He is here with me now, right this minute. I am not traveling alone. Why am I allowing myself to stay in a state of worry and anger instead of praying? That was easier said than done, because I was still furious. I began to pray anyway.

I began by thanking God for the things I was thankful for. I was thankful for our safe travel up until then, and thankful for the family and friends that we will be spending time with. I was thankful that I had the opportunity to explore new regions of our beautiful country and to have new adventures to look forward to. I was thankful that my mother's health was good enough that she could enjoy coming on holidays with us, and thankful that my husband and her got along splendidly and enjoyed each other's company well enough that he encouraged her to join us on holidays. I was thankful that tomorrow was a new day. Most of all, I was thankful that I can come to our Lord in prayer any time at all, any single minute of any given day, with absolutely any issue, big or small, and ask Him for help, confident that He has heard my prayer and will help me.

I had been worrying for nothing.

Thank you Heavenly Father, for being with me in the midst of my self-created emotional turmoil.

Ephesians 4: 26, 27

"And don't sin by letting anger control you. Don't let the sun go down while you are still angry, for anger gives a foothold to the devil."

* * *

Whether at work or at play, our loving Father is always with us. One of my favorite things about being a cashier was the wide assortment of people whom I had the opportunity to interact with on every single shift. My job was certainly never boring. I never knew who was going to walk through the doors next.

There was always a wide variety of customers to serve. Some individuals seemed to always be in a perpetual hurry, galloping in and out at top speed every time I saw them. They walked fast, they spoke fast, and they quickly made decisions about what to buy. Others seemed to have all the time in the world, every single day. They were never in a hurry, and chatted leisurely with other customers while shopping, then took time to chat with me at the till also. Some people spoke only enough words to conduct the immediate business transaction at hand, while others liked to stand at the till and visit, making small talk as long as time would allow, discussing happenings around our little town. Some people were honest and I never felt that I had to watch them at all. There were also those acted suspicious while they walked around and 'shopped', whom I tried to watch very closely. Some individuals were very easy going, and nothing seemed to rattle them, while others were demanding and acted quite indignant if they experienced any inconvenience whatsoever while they were being served. Children and teenagers were always high energy and extremely enjoyable to be around. A few people, however, were moody and therefore just plain unpredictable.

While I was working at the local gas station, two such colorful, local characters used to always come in together, very regularly on my shifts. They were totally unpredictable. On good days, they loitered around for long periods of time, playing the lottery and chatting leisurely with me. Other times, they came bolting in thought the doors very quickly, sometimes cutting in front of other customers already in line. In this mood, they sometimes demanded instant service because they "were regular customers and in a hurry." This created a problem on more than one occasion, and I found this particular mood of theirs to be very annoying to deal with on a regular basis. I could usually tell what mood they were in by their body language and facial expressions as soon as they walked in through the front door.

One waitress in town, who worked at a local restaurant, mentioned to me one day that this particular pair liked to come in when I was working because I was nice to them, and that they even considered me to be a rather good friend. I was surprised to hear that, because I had never thought of them as friends. To be perfectly honest, I rather dreaded seeing them walking in through the door while I was working, because they could be extremely demanding if they took notion to be. Being told that they liked me and considered me to be a friend only made me feel guilty about the negative way that I was feeling about them. Yes, I knew from Bible Study and church that we are all brothers and sisters in Christ, and that God loves each and every one of us equally, but I just simply found these two particular customers extremely difficult to deal with. For my part, 'love' was entirely out of the question. The most I could usually muster up during a transaction was civil tolerance.

Early one morning I had just experienced a 'gas and dash', (a driver who drove off without paying for fuel after putting fuel in their vehicle), and my boss and I were standing at the till discussing what we could remember about the vehicle and driver, and what our next immediate step was going to be. I was feeling entirely disheartened with thieving humanity, and annoyed this just happened on my shift.

In my peripheral vision, I saw two customers come in and stand in front of the till, waiting for service. The matter at hand was more pressing, however, and I took almost a full minute to finish my conversation with my boss before I turned my attention to the customers. When I looked up to see who was standing in front of me, it was none other than my demanding duo.

I thought, "Great! This is just what I need right now! These two! They are going to tear a strip right off me."

Of all people to have ignored for almost a full minute, it was my misfortune that it should happen to be these two. They would surely give me a piece of their mind about the slow service, and not be delicate in their choice of words, either. They had been very quick in the past to let me know when they were displeased with any aspect of my service, what so ever.

While I instantly braced myself mentally preparing to deal with them, so very immediately after facing the disheartening gas and dash just minutes prior, a gentle voice tenderly said, *"Be thankful for the honest ones."*

Honest ones? I had been so busy looking at what I considered to be their faults that I never gave a single thought to their positive qualities.

Several specific incidents came to my mind immediately. In these prior transactions, they would each buy several scratch tickets, which I counted out and passed to them. They would pay me, and sometimes leave to have coffee elsewhere and scratch their tickets, or sometimes they would take the scratch tickets to the lottery table a few feet away and scratch them there. A few times, however, one or the other would return to the till and hand me back an unscratched ticket, telling me that I had accidently passed them more tickets than what they had paid for, by mistake. New tickets sometimes stuck together, and I had not noticed when I was counting them out. Sometimes they would return unscratched tickets an hour or more after they purchased them, but they did come back and rectify my mistake. Yes, they were definitely honest citizens. I had to give them that. They were both a little quirky perhaps, but I could attest to the fact that they were definitely honest.

I looked at them, standing in front of my till, in a totally different light. They were not just two customers who were demanding and outspoken, whom I should dread to see coming in through the door. They had their good qualities, too. Why had I not been focusing on that? Our transaction went smoothly, despite their having to wait for service, and I had food for thought to work on.

How many other times and with how many other people had I focused on what I considered to be negative qualities when there were so many positive ones to enjoy instead?

1 Thessalonians 5:18
"Be thankful in all circumstances, for this is God's will for you who belong to Christ Jesus."

* * *

Before pre-paying for fuel became mandatory in British Columbia, there came a time that we began to experience a rash of 'gas and dash' incidents at our station. The price of fuel was climbing rapidly as the summer months and busy long weekends approached. It seemed that almost every time I worked a set of four days (we worked four days on and four days off), I would experience at least one gas and dash, usually on one of my morning shifts when it was the busiest with shift change workers from the copper mine seventeen kilometers away. I was a conscientious employee, and I began to find this situation very stressful, not to mention extremely frustrating.

The 'gas and dashes' continued to happen periodically, and I was beginning to feel very disheartened and thinking that doing my best was simply not good enough in this case. To make matters worse, I was beginning to take it personally, even though I knew that it was a rather common occurrence at any given gas station, on any given shift around the country. They happened everywhere, to anyone who worked in these places. That gave me no comfort, and my own situation bothered me to the point where I seriously contemplated applying for a different job.

One morning, however, out of the clear blue, my boss approached me and said something like, "I realize that I haven't done enough to help you with this."

I felt a huge sense of relief sweep over me, and we spent some time talking. He had some good ideas as to how to approach the problem, and together we discussed several options. He was quiet and sincere, and I had a feeling that God had brought my problem to his attention, and encouraged him to help me.

Galatians 6:2, 3
"Share each other's burdens, and in this way, obey the law of Christ."

Chapter 22

A Specific Purpose

6:00 a.m. Sunday, Oct. 16, 2006

Today, as I write, it is Sunday morning and I am at work at the local Petro Can station. At 5 a.m. this morning on my way to work, I noticed the price of gas on the huge sign outside - 88.9 cents per liter. It must have come down in price from 90.9 yesterday when I was at work on morning shift.

At about 6:30 am this morning, one customer came in and said, "I want some of your 38 cent gas."

"Pardon me?" was my very surprised answer.

"Just what your sign outside says - 38 cents a liter."

I looked out the window and sure enough, there in black and white, the sign reads '38.9', clear as a bell. I was shocked! I had just looked at that exact sign an hour and a half ago when I pulled into the parking lot at work, to begin my shift, and had specifically noticed that the price read 88.9.

This sign is set atop steel posts approximately 20 feet above the ground. The prices have to be changed manually. The manager physically gets our extension ladder from the inside storage area, carries it outside to the sign, leans it against the steel pole, and climbs up to the lighted casing of the sign. Then he manually lifts out the number card (or cards) with the old price and replaces it with the correct card(s), therefore displaying the new price. These cards are kept in the office, near to where the till is.

I did not even know how to react to what my eyes were seeing and what my customer was telling me, let alone know what to say. I have absolutely no idea why the sign read as it did. I knew for a fact that it has not been manually changed, because I was the only one here at work. Yet there it sits, lit up against the morning sky, the numbers different than they were an hour-and-a-half ago when I came to work. I *knew* that no one has touched them.

Two more customers come in later, at separate times, each also pointing out the 38.9 cent gas. After they gas up and leave, each time I walked outside and stared at and studied the massive out door sign very carefully. It definitely reads 38.9. The backlight is fully lit and not shaded, and the numbers are correct, that is definitely a 3 up there instead of an 8. There's something strange going on this morning. I figure that my father is playing tricks on me from the afterlife place where he is at. He used to like playing tricks. There can be no other explanation.

Sunday mornings are generally quiet at work for the first few hours except for shift change with the local mine workers. This morning, after I caught up on my morning duties and the shift change ended, I took out a sheet of paper to draw some sketches on while it was momentarily quiet. Nothing I sketched seemed to be coming together, and drawing just somehow didn't feel right. It actually felt very awkward, which was very unusual, because I love to draw. So I decided that it was not the time or place to draw. None of the magazines or newspapers appealed to me to read, and it was still very quiet with customers. I had nothing to do, or at least nothing that I wanted to do.

Then came that loud, nagging feeling *–again–* that I have been experiencing lately: 'Write something – right now!'

What on earth am I supposed to write?

So I took the piece of paper that I had intended to draw on, sat quietly, and an idea came to me, a memory from my past. I jotted it down. Not in any detail, just the basic incident. Then another one and another one, specific memories popped into my mind. I just keep jotting words down as they had come to me.

There! This just feels *so* right, even though I don't have a clue where this is all headed. This is exactly what I am supposed to be doing this morning. I had that 'gut feeling' that tells me that what I am doing at this exact moment is 100% correct. Since I'm at work this Sunday morning and can't go to church to worship, I feel as though I am at least following God's gentle little nudge on His day, as much as I am able to from where I'm at.

When my small drawing sheet was full of random notes, I jotted down incidents as they come to me, as I thought of them, on little sticky yellow note pads. At a quiet time in between jottings of memories, I evaluate where I am in my life right now.

I was going to go to attend Cursillo in 2 weeks. It is an Anglican weekend retreat that my friend and my Anglican pastor have graciously sponsored me for. Lately I've been praying for direction in my life. I was hitting a low point with pursuing my Christian walk and was entertaining thoughts of quitting going to church altogether, and just living a regular life with my atheist husband. We would be on the same page again, if I did that. Life would be easier. I've never been to a retreat before, but it sounds like it could be fun. Hopefully I will gain some clarity while I am there.

But lately, I was feeling very strongly that God wanted me to write. There have even been two or three people that have specifically said to me, during innocent conversations, "You should write."

It is almost eerie to hear that out loud from someone else while I am privately entertaining the same idea, but not saying a word about it to anyone else. However, I am not a writer. For starters, I really have nothing to write about. I enjoy writing personal letters to my friends and family, but that is about it. I am a self-taught painter. I am pretty sure that art is my gift from God, not writing.

Eventually, business begins to pick up and I realize that I have to put my scraps of notes away and focus entirely on work for the rest of my shift. I was feeling absolutely positive that what I did that morning (in jotting down a few memories on scraps of paper) was the right thing to do!

I glance at the clock. It's 8:35 a.m. I look outside and the pricing sign reads 88.9 again, clear as a bell.

Amazing!

The outdoor price sign twenty feet off the ground is back like it was when I arrived at work at three and a half hours ago, at 5 a.m.

I had an unexplainable peaceful feeling that I am one in harmony with God's will for me. This euphoric feeling that I experienced is all because I have merely jotted down some of my earlier life's memories down on yellow sticky notes and a little drawing paper. I felt as though God has somehow used the outdoor sign this morning as a specific sign to me to make me pay attention to His nudges.

I must admit that I do not particularly like the idea of trying to write a book, and I feel scared to death to write about my own personal life because I prefer to remain extremely private about my own affairs. But who am I to argue with God about the direction He is leading me in?

I really cannot imagine where this could possibly be headed. Surely He is not really going to expect me to go through with this.

Psalm 119:73

"You made me; you created me.

Now give me the sense to follow your commands."

Nov. 25, 2006

I have started writing in a journal. Today I have just finishing copying the last of my scribbles from loose pages and yellow sticky notes (that I jotted down at Petro Can that Sunday morning this project began) into a journal. That peaceful feeling I experienced the first time I jotted notes down keeps occurring every single time that I write. I have also remembered two more incidents to make notes of.

I was thinking about that as I went to bed. There is such absolute peace in my soul when I write down my memories that there is absolutely no doubt in my mind that this is definitely God's will for me right now, without question. What I am feeling must be the "peace that passes all understanding" that is mentioned in the church service every Sunday. I was feeling very pleased with myself for figuring that out, and turned out the light to go to sleep.

Just as I am dozing off, I hear a loving voice again, telling me very specifically, *"Voices and Visions - that is to be the title of this book."*

Talk about absolute confirmation!

I definitely have to go through with writing this book about my life. Now I am even given the title. The title is totally perfect, because that is exactly this book is all about. It is my personal walk in which I discover our Lord; His voice which I am privileged to hear, and the visions He has freely shown to me. Thank you, Heavenly Father, for your clarity on this.

Apparently it is to be a book, too, not a magazine article or a pamphlet, but an actual, whole book.

Good grief! What next?

I lay in bed and think about how to approach this mammoth job of which I know absolutely nothing about. I am completely unqualified to write a book, and I know utterly nothing about publishing a book.

I have to trust that I will be shown the steps in order, as I have need of them. I did not turn on the light and write down the title of the book immediately after I heard the voice. After all, I could *never* forget something so specific (and short). The next morning, however, I was not sure if I was told 'Voices and Visions' or 'Visions and Voices.'

Yet again, the flesh is so weak. Will I ever learn? It would have taken me less than sixty seconds, one mere minute, to turn on the bedside lamp and jot those three words down. I will have to trust that when the time comes, however that is going to happen, God will nudge me into knowing His desire for the title, *again*.

I must admit that I was and maybe still am a bit of a reluctant servant. In the months to come, which ended up turning into several years, I would write things down and try to get them into some sort of semblance of a book. Many times I felt very discouraged and did not want to continue. Always, when I was ready to quit, inspiration would appear from what seemed out of nowhere. Several times I would just be talking to different friends or neighbors, and they would suggest that I should write, out of the clear blue. They had absolutely no idea that I was already in the process of writing a book.

The most amazing encouragement arrived from a woman I have never met. Betty thought I would be interested in a journal that her sister-in-law kept and had shared with her. With permission, she shared it with me. I was privileged and delighted to read the private words of one other lady whom God spoke direct words to, at different circumstances in her life. I found it to be extremely encouraging knowing that I am not alone in this experience.

God is always good, kind, loving, and patient. Oh yes - and she also received one 'message' that started out as a dream in which the phone rang and she answered it.

It keeps being confirmed to me again and again how important it is to share positive experiences with each other and encourage each other, because this helps us to lift each other up in spirit.

All glory be to God.

Acts 20:24

"But my life is worth nothing to me unless I use it for finishing the work assigned me by the Lord Jesus – the work of telling others the Good News about the wonderful grace of God."

EPILOGUE

I have been very fortunate in my life. God has always been with me. He has always been beside me, and has been watching over me long before I knew Him and was able to acknowledge that He existed.

Thank-you, Heavenly Father, for all the blessings you freely bestow upon me that I am aware of, and also for the many more which go unnoticed by me in my busy day. Thank you for being a loving Father who is always with us.

In the past, you have freely opened my "eyes" to many insights, and have literally spoken your Word directly to my heart. I have lived and experienced life without you, and have I lived and experienced life with you.

I will never walk alone again.

This book is proof that with God's divine power working in and through us and guiding us, we can do more than we ever could ever ask or imagine.

To God be all the glory!

You, precious child of God, who are holding this book in your hand right now, and have taken your valuable time to read it, know and accept the fact that God loves you. You are His creation and He will always love His creation.

This is my prayer for you, today and every day:

Numbers 6: 24-26:
"May the Lord bless you
and protect you
May the Lord smile upon you
and be gracious to you
May the Lord show you his favor
and give you his peace.
Amen"

Bible Study Notes

My own interpretations for this Bible Study are based upon the clear explanations offered by professionals in the Life Application Study Bible.

They have not been quoted verbatim but have been paraphrased.

Chapter 1

Genesis 1:26, 27 "Then God said, 'Let us make human beings in our image, to be like ourselves. They will reign over the fish in the sea, the birds in the sky, the livestock, all the wild animals on the earth, and the small animals that scurry along the ground.'
So God created human beings in his own image.
In the image of God he created them'
Male and female he created them."

The 'us' and 'our image' refers to God, Jesus Christ, and the Holy Spirit (the Trinity). Creativity is work, and God's work includes creating you. God is pleased with and loves His creation, for **Genesis 1:31** states, **"Then God looked over all He had made, and He saw that it was very good..."** You are valuable to Him just the way you are. Although society places a high value on achievements, possessions, physical looks or public acclaim, we can rest assured that our self-worth comes from sharing God's characteristics, such as reasoning, creativity, speech and self-determination. Although God has no physical body, we reflect being created in His image by our ability to love, have patience, show kindness and forgiveness, and be faithful.

God expects us to be careful with and responsible for the environment and creatures that He created.

Society has made man exalted and 'more important' than woman, not God.

Chapter 2

Jeremiah 1:5 (The Lord's message) "I knew you before I formed you in your mother's womb. Before you were born, I set you apart...."

God has planned for you and known you long before you were even conceived. You are valuable to Him, and He has a purpose for your life. Many people throughout history in the Bible were called to do specific tasks for God. All believers are called to love, obey and serve God until His guidance becomes clearer on what He wants you to do specifically. Accept your tasks cheerfully and work at them with diligence and the best of your ability for the glory of God.

Chapter 3

Ephesians 6:10-12 "A final word: Be strong in the Lord and in His mighty power. Put on all of God's armor so that you will be able to stand firm against all strategies of the devil. For we are not fighting against flesh and blood enemies, but against evil rulers and authorities of the unseen world, against mighty powers in this dark world, and against evil spirits in the heavenly places."

There is a continuous spiritual battle going on all around us, and evil forces are very real. We can arm ourselves, however, with the supernatural power of the Holy Spirit who resides within us, and rely on God's strength to help us.

Chapter 4

Luke 10:21,22 "At that same time Jesus was filled with the joy of the Holy Spirit, and he said, 'O Father, Lord of heaven and earth, thank you for hiding these things from those who think themselves wise and clever, and for revealing them to the childlike. Yes, Father, it pleased you to do it this way. My Father has entrusted everything to me. No one truly knows the Son except the Father, and no one truly knows the Father except the Son and those to whom the Son chooses to reveal him.' "

Spiritual truth is for everyone alike, and Jesus is thanking God that we all have access to it. Being wise in one's own eyes is spiritual pride, and Jesus is opposed to that. Those who come to Him with childlike trust can understand God more clearly. Jesus explained God's love for us through stories, teachings, and by example of how He lived his own life while here on earth. Studying Jesus' actions, principals, and attitudes will help us to understand God more clearly.

Chapter 5

Romans 7:15- 17, 22, 23 "I don't really understand myself, for I want to do what is right, but I don't do it. Instead, I do what I hate. But if I know that what I am doing is wrong, this shows that I agree that the law is good. So I am not the one doing wrong; it is the sin living in me that does it. ...I love God's law with all my heart. But there is another power within me that is at war with my mind. This power makes me a slave to the sin that is still within me."

Every single person is tempted to sin sometimes (lie, steal, cheat, to name just a few). We are powerless to fight sin with our own strength, but with the Spirit's help we can succeed. Christians are tempted the same as everyone else. It is a lifelong process to become like Jesus Christ and that is living without sin.

Psalm 34:18 "The Lord is close to the brokenhearted;
He rescues those whose spirits are crushed."

He loves us and knows everything that we are going through. He never leaves us. When our spirits are crushed by circumstances in our lives, it is with His loving help that we recover.

Chapter 6

Ephesians 2:12 "In those days, you were living apart from Christ. ...You lived in this world without God and without hope."

Believing in our living God gives us hope, and this hope breaks down walls of prejudice so that everyone who believes in Him from all walks of life, are united together into one body of believers.

Chapter 7

Psalm 91:11, 12 "For He will order his angels to protect you wherever you go. They will hold you up with their hands so you won't even hurt your foot on a stone."

One of the jobs that guardian angels have is to watch over us. It is comforting to know that even in times of great stress and fear, God is watching over us.

Chapter 8

Ecclesiastes 3:11 "Yet God has made everything beautiful for its own time. He has planted eternity in the human heart, but even so, people cannot see the whole scope of God's work from beginning to end."

Our spiritual thirst comes from being created in God's image, and therefore only a personal relationship with God can truly satisfy us. We have eternal value in Him and to Him, because are a part of His eternal plan. Our restlessness is a result of being separated from Him.

Even though we cannot comprehend His plans, we can trust Him fully and do the work on earth that He has set before us. He is the beginning and the end, and He never changes.

Proverbs 14:12 *"There is a path before each person that seems right, but in the end it leads to death."*

Spiritual death can be the result of the choices we make. Some easy choices allow us to be lazy or do not require any lifestyle changes, whereas some right choices often require self-sacrifice and hard work on our part.

Acts 7:55, 56 *"But Stephen, full of the Holy Spirit, gazed steadily into heaven and saw the glory of God, and he saw Jesus standing in the place of honor at God's right hand."*

Jesus was condemned to death for blasphemy by the Jewish leaders. Stephen's vision of Jesus also angered the Jewish leaders, so he, too, was dragged out and killed. Many people will not want to hear us witnessing about Christ, either, and will try to silence us. We still need to continue to honor God with our actions and words, however. Paul became the world's greatest missionary after being profoundly impacted by Stephen's death. Those who oppose us strongly now may later turn to Jesus Christ.

Chapter 9

2 Corinthians 11:14 "...Even Satan disguises himself as an angel of light."

Satan is a master deceiver who disguises himself cleverly to appear to be good, attractive, and moral. Some leaders today lead innocent people into cults and alienate them from their families. A true leader who is a follower of Christ will not lead anyone into immorality or a deceitful lifestyle. Their own lifestyle will be consistent with biblical morals and their teachings will confirm scripture. They will proclaim that Jesus Christ is God, who came down to earth to save us from our sins. We have to be careful not to be deceived by outward appearances.

Chapter 10

Luke 15:3-7 "So Jesus told them this story: 'If a man has a hundred sheep and one of them gets lost, what will he do? Won't he leave the ninety-nine others in the wilderness and go to search for the one that is lost until he finds it? And when he has found it, he will joyfully carry it home on his shoulders. When he arrives, he will call together his friends and neighbors, saying, 'Rejoice with me because I have found my lost sheep.' In the same way, there is more joy in heaven over one lost sinner who repents and returns to God than over ninety-nine others who are righteous and haven't strayed away.' "

Jesus told this parable to show us how valuable we are to God: we are the sheep, He is the shepherd. Because God loves each one of us, His creation, He rejoices when we are reunited with Him. The ninety nine sheep that are together are safe, but the lost one is alone and in danger. You are valuable to God, and He seeks you out individually so that you, too, may become one of His flock. God sought you before you were a believer, and He joyfully forgives all your sins because of His extraordinary love for you.

Chapter 11

Romans 12:2 "Don't copy the behavior and customs of this world, but let God transform you into a new person by changing the way you think. Then you will learn to know God's will for you, which is good and pleasing and perfect."

It is only when we begin to think differently that we will begin to speak and act differently. Our actions and words result from our thoughts. God's plans for us are good and pleasing and perfect, and He wants only what is best for us. In contrast, the ways of the world are selfish and corrupting, even though they may seem inviting and exciting. The Holy Spirit, who lives within us, renews and reeducates our minds so that we can avoid being proud, covetous, selfish, stubborn, and arrogant.

Chapter 12

1 Thessalonians 5:12, 13 "Dear brothers and sisters, honor those who are your leaders in the Lord's work. They work hard among you and give you spiritual guidance. Show them great respect and wholehearted love because of their work. And live peacefully with each other."

We can honor our pastors and church leaders by thanking them for their ministry, and letting them know how their sermons affect our lives in a positive way. They are actively working at being God's hands and feet here on earth by ministering to us, just as Jesus ministered to those around Him. By expressing our appreciation for their leadership and teaching, we also encourage them in their line of work.

Chapter 13

Matthew 18:20 "For where two or three gather together as my followers, I (Jesus) am there among them."

243

When we pray together sincerely with other believers, the Holy Spirit within us (who is one part of the trinity and therefore directly residing in God and Jesus Christ as well as us) clarifies our requests and brings them in line with God's will for us in that matter. These prayers are much more powerful than thousands of people who agree superficially, without God's guidance.

Chapter 14

Romans 8:26, 27 "And the Holy Spirit helps us in our weakness. For example, we don't know what God wants us to pray for. But the Holy Spirit prays for us with groanings that cannot be expressed in words. And the Father who knows all hearts knows what the Spirit is saying, for the Spirit pleads for us believers in harmony with God's own will."

When you are feeling emotionally overwhelmed by circumstances to the point where you cannot think clearly and rationally enough to even pray with clarity, the Holy Spirit within you will intercede and pray with you and for you, in harmony with God's own will. We do not have to try and cope with problems on our own. God will always do what is best for us.

Chapter 15

Matthew 11:28-30 "Then Jesus said, 'Come to me, all of you, who are weary and carry heavy burdens, and I will give you rest. Take my yoke upon you. Let me teach you, because I am humble and gentle at heart, and you will find rest for your souls. For my yoke is easy to bear, and the burden I give you is light.' "

The dictionary describes a yoke as, 'a wooden frame or bar with loops at either end, fitted around the necks of a pair of oxen for harnessing them together,' (enabling them to work together). We can work together with Jesus through prayer. He already died for us so that we could be free in His love and experience rest in all circumstances, rather than feel that we have to carry the weight of the world upon our shoulders alone. "Our burden" will be light, because He is a powerful partner and more weight will fall upon His shoulders than our own.

Romans 5:3-5 "We can rejoice, too, when we run into problems and trials, for we know that they help us develop endurance. And endurance develops strength of character, and character strengthens our confident hope of salvation. And this hope will not lead to disappointment. For we know how dearly God loves us, because He has given us the Holy Spirit to fill our hearts with His love."

As Christians, although we feel God's comforting presence in our lives, we also face problems and pressures. We grow spiritually by learning to

245

depend on God's power to help us deal with smaller issues as well as larger tribulations, rather than feel discouraged and helpless. Perseverance to experience God's peace in our lives during trials helps to develop our strength of character, deepen our trust in God, and help us to feel confident about our future. We can thank God and rejoice in the fact that each experience can be dealt with in His strength, and is an opportunity for our own spiritual growth.

Chapter 16

Ephesians 2:8-10 "God saved you by His grace when you believed. And you can't take credit for this; it is a gift from God. Salvation is not a reward for the good things we have done, so none of us can boast about it. For we are God's masterpiece. He created us new in Christ Jesus, so we can do the good things He planned for us long ago."

In the very beginning, we were created in God's own image, with an ability to think, reason, be creative, and have feelings. God loves His creation, and that includes you and me. This fact alone is reason to celebrate life and make a conscious effort, if need be, to experience feelings of joy. God *wants* us to be happy and stable in His strength, rather than be up one day and down the next. We are free to do the good things He planned for us long ago, such as treat others with respect, kindness, love and gentleness. Our 'being saved' by Jesus is not for our own benefit only, but gives us an opportunity to serve Christ and build up His church.

'We already know how much God loves us, and that frees us up to love others.'

Because you are God's masterpiece, you must also treat yourself with respect and take proper care of yourself.

Psalm 5:1, 2 "O Lord, hear me as I pray, pay attention to my groaning. Listen to my cry for help, my King and my God, for I pray to no one but you."

God is a living God who is always with us, and therefore can always help us in dire circumstances even when we feel like there seems to be no way out. He will often prompt other people to come to our rescue, and they may not even be aware of the significance of their actions. He hears every single one of our prayers and pleadings, and always answers in one of three ways: yes, no, or not yet – wait.

Developing a good habit of prayer every single day is very rewarding. When we pray to Him earnestly each morning and commit the whole day to Him, we build a strong relationship with Him. We also need to study His Word (the Bible) to learn how to live like Jesus.

Chapter 17

Galatians 5:14, 15 "For the whole law can be summed up in this one command: 'Love your neighbors as yourself.' But if you are always biting and devouring one another, watch out. Beware of destroying one another."

It is easy to see other people's faults and become critical of them. Dwelling on negative thoughts results in acting and speaking in a negative manner, and destroys our own joy rapidly. It is often easier to lash out in anger and focus on others' shortcomings rather than their strengths. It also prompts others to retaliate in a like manner, and a vicious, negative cycle begins. Some people put others down in order to feel better about themselves. However, Jesus commands us to love others as you love yourself (Matthew 22:39). We can just as easily build a positive atmosphere around us in which we can confront problems in a loving manner.

2 Corinthians 6: 14, 15 "Don't team up with those who are unbelievers. How can righteousness be a partner with wickedness? How can light live with darkness? ...How can a believer be a partner with an unbeliever?"

Here the Apostle Paul is concerned that if believers partner in marriage to unbelievers, they may have to compromise their beliefs, and this, in turn, will weaken their Christian integrity, standards, or commitment. They may feel forced to divide their loyalties. There is more strength in unity than in disagreement.

John 14:15-17 "If you love me, obey my commandments. And I will ask the Father, and He will give you another Advocate, who will never leave you. He is the Holy Spirit, who leads into all truth. The world cannot receive Him, because it isn't looking for Him, and doesn't recognize Him. But you know Him, because He lives with you now and later will be in you."

The Holy Spirit is a powerful person who is on our side. His presence within us helps us to live as God wants us to live. With faith, we can confidently call upon His power to help us each day in all circumstances. It is comforting to know that He will never leave us and that He leads us into all truth. With His guidance, we can look at life in a whole new way.

Chapter 18

Ephesians 1:16, 17 "I have not stopped thanking God for you. I pray for you constantly, asking God, the glorious Father of our Lord Jesus

Christ, to give you spiritual wisdom and insight so that you might grow in your knowledge of God."

Even though the Holy Spirit lives within us, we can only grow in our knowledge of God by spending time with Him: in prayer, in church, discussing His Word with other believers, and in studying the Bible. There are no short cuts. We need to study Jesus' life in the Bible by reading the gospels of Matthew, Mark, Luke and John, and sincerely think about what you are reading. As we grow in the knowledge of God, our lives will change as we react differently to situations around us. Jesus' life is our example to follow.

Chapter 19

Philippians 4:8, 9 "And now, dear brothers and sisters, one final thing. Fix your thoughts on what is true, and honorable, and right, and pure, and lovely, and admirable. Think about things that are excellent and worthy of praise. Keep putting into practice all you learned and received from me – everything you heard from me and saw me doing. Then the God of peace will be with you."

God's Word is for everybody. He is interested in being active in your life, and all you need to do is to begin spending time with Him in prayer and learning His Word. We all need to practice focusing on things that are true, honorable, right, pure, lovely and admirable. Perhaps your reading material, conversations, TV shows, internet interests, books, movies, and magazines are harmful and need to be examined. What are you putting into your mind? Replace it with God's wholesome material, and ask God to help you focus on what is pure and good. Our studying of God's Word must lead to obedience.

Chapter 20

Exodus 4:1 "But Moses protested again, 'What if they won't believe me or listen to me? What if they say, 'The Lord never appeared to you?'"

Moses was apprehensive and reluctant, worrying about how the people would respond to him. Speaking out for God in today's world is still not popular, nor even accepted kindly. Although it takes great courage to do so, God gives us the strength, confidence and power to carry out the work that He has assigned us to do here on earth.

Romans 10:14, 15 "But how can they call on Him to save them unless they believe in Him? And how can they believe in Him if they have never heard about Him? And how can they hear about Him unless someone tells them? And how will anyone go and tell them without being sent? That is why the Scriptures say, 'How beautiful are the feet of messengers who bring good news.' "

In order to effectively tell someone about Jesus Christ, we need to be prepared to answer questions and provide explanations to nonbelievers who may not have an understanding about God's Word. It is not enough to just be a good example. We need to be able speak clearly about our beliefs to promote the gospel. How will our loved ones, neighbors, and friends hear God's message unless someone tells them? Be willing to follow God's prompting about speaking to others.

Chapter 21

Matthew 7:1, 3-5 "Do not judge others, and you will not be judged... And why worry about a speck in your friend's eye when you have a log in your own? How can you think of saying to your friend, 'Let me help you get rid of that speck in your eye', when you can't see past the log in your own eye? Hypocrite! First get rid of the log in your own eye; then you will see well enough to deal with the speck in your friend's eye."

When somebody does something that bothers us, Jesus tells us to check our motives. Sometimes we put other people down just to build ourselves up in our own minds, or else we think that kind of talk will make us look better to whom we are speaking with at the time. Very often it is our own same habits and actions that we don't like but which we see magnified in other people. It is easier to criticize and judge them and excuse our own same actions. Our job is to lovingly forgive and help others. We also need to avoid all gossip about others, for believing gossip may affect how we act towards those who are gossiped about.

* * *

1 Corinthians 6:19, 20 "Don't you realize that your body is the temple of the Holy Spirit, who lives in you and was given to you by God? You do not belong to yourself, for God bought you with a high price. So you must honor God with your body."

We need to take care of ourselves in body and in spirit. Spiritually, we need to live in a manner that is pleasing to God. Physically, we need to pay attention to healthy choices and treat our bodies as the temple of the Holy Spirit which the Bible clearly states that it is.

* * *

Isaiah 30:21 "Your own ears will hear Him. Right behind you a voice will say, 'This is the way you should go,' whether to the right or to the left."

In this passage, God is correcting the people of Jerusalem when He sees that they are straying from His path. He does the same for us today, and it is for our own benefit that He lovingly speaks to our hearts. It is up to us to take the initiative to follow Him.

* * *

Daniel 10: 7 "Only I, Daniel, saw this vision. The men with me saw nothing, but they were suddenly terrified and ran away to hide."

God is capable of blocking one person's eyes and opening another's while people are physically in close proximity. He has specific jobs and purposes for each one of us, and they are all different. You need only to concentrate on the job He has given to you. We are all gifted in different ways.

* * *

Ephesians 4: 26, 27 "And 'don't sin by letting anger control you.' Don't let the sun go down while you are still angry, for anger gives a foothold to the devil."

All of us are going to get angry some times. When we feel angry, we should not speak and act thoughtlessly, nor should we bottle it up. These reactions harm relationships, hurt others, or make us bitter. Paul tells us to immediately deal with our feelings of anger in a proper manner so that our relationships are not jeopardized. By holding onto anger, we hurt ourselves most.

* * *

1 Thessalonians 5:18 "Be thankful in all circumstances, for this is God's will for you who belong to Christ Jesus."

We need to differentiate and be thankful *in* all circumstances, not *for* all circumstances. We can always be thankful that God is present in our lives every minute of every day, and He will help us accomplish something good from the distress of what negative issue we are dealing with.

* * *

Galatians 6: 2, 3 "Share each other's burdens, and in this way obey the law of Christ."

None of us are so independent that we do not need help from others. In the same way, we should also freely help others who we see struggling. We were created to use our diversity of gifts and talents to help and support each other, thus creating a strong community.

Chapter 22

Psalm 119:73 *"You made me; you created me. Now give me the sense to follow your commands."*

We need to use our God-given common sense to make intelligent and wise choices in our lives.

Acts 20:24 *"But my life is worth nothing to me unless I use it for finishing the work assigned me by the Lord Jesus – the work of telling others the Good News about the wonderful grace of God."*

Paul was the greatest missionary who ever lived because his sole focus and goal in life was to tell others about Jesus Christ. God is still looking for individuals to centralize their energy on whichever specific task He has given them to do.

We often feel that unless we are getting recognition from others, having fun, and enjoying money, that our lives are unsuccessful. Paul, however, considered that using his life to do God's work was the most important thing that he could ever do. He was more concerned about what he put into life rather than what he got out of life. Which is more important to you?

Epilogue

Numbers 6:24-26 "May the Lord bless you and protect you. May the Lord smile on you and be gracious to you. May the Lord show you His favor and give you His peace."

We can love and encourage others by praying for them. This ancient blessing asks for God to bless and protect those whom we pray for. It asks Him to be pleased with them (smile upon), and be merciful and compassionate to them (gracious). It asks Him to give them His approval (favor) and His peace. This prayer models one way in which we can care for each other.

ACKNOWLEDGEMENTS

This book would never have been written and published without the help of many good and wonderful people who are a very important part of my life.

Thank you to my beautiful friend and neighbor, Georgi Abbott. You are a self-published author of a series of excellently written, informative, and entertaining books about your eccentric pet, Pickles the Parrot. Without your help, I don't know if this book would never have been published. You have admirable patience with researching self-publishing sites on the internet, and have freely given your time to help me get published, when I did not even have so much as a single clue as to how to begin this mammoth task. Thank you, also, for your help and wisdom with formatting this book, and sharing your resources with me. Your vast knowledge about publishing solid cover books as well as e-books, and your kindness to help me 'jump through all the hoops' are highly praiseworthy. I had absolutely no idea of the amount of work involved with publishing, but you have patiently walked me through each and every step. Your quaint words of encouragement when I was dragging my feet also got me back on track and busy again. I sincerely appreciate everything you have helped me with, and I can never thank you enough. I feel like God has placed you in my neighborhood strictly for me!

Thank you to my e-mail friend, Tamber. You have turned my painting into a one of a kind designer book cover with your artistic flair and computer savvy. You have also carefully edited this book for me, and made knowledgeable and valuable suggestions where I overlooked the obvious. Although computers have spell check and grammar check, I greatly appreciate you taking the time to go over this book for me with a fine tooth comb and make sure that it is written clearly and easy to understand.

Thank you to my beautiful daughter Kristina for allowing me to write about and share, from your private life, what you went through as a result of your accidents. For the first time in my life, since you were born, I was forced to leave you entirely in the care of health professionals and in God's hands. I appreciate that you are willing to let me share your personal story with others in this book. You have suffered extensive injuries in your younger years, and thanks be to God, you have recovered fully, more than I ever dared to hope for. Thank you, also, for the fun 'photo shoots' that we went on, trying to get one good picture for the cover of this book. You are truly a blessing to me.

Thank you to my beautiful daughter Adele for allowing me to write about and share a very personal portion of your life while you were going through an extremely trying time. I had to give you to God completely, and trust that He would help you to heal from a devastating illness that I was powerless to help you fight. Thanks be to God, you have been healed completely. I am grateful that you have the self-confidence and courage to let your story be told here. You are truly a blessing to me.

Thank you to my unique friend and mentor, Betty White, who has known me since before I began my Christian walk. You have been with me on every single step of this journey, and I am thankful for your wise guidance. You encouraged me to begin writing this book and also many times during the process when I felt disheartened about continuing. I have phoned you countless times to ask your advice on a section I had written, knowing that you would tell me honesty if the words I used conveyed the message as intended. Thank you for being sensitive to the time and space that I needed, over the years, to learn to exercise my varying degrees of faith and to turn my life around. You have wisely pointed out God's promises to me that are written in the Bible and helped me to realize that the written Word in the Bible is personal, for each and every one of us, even me. You have been a true blessing in my life.

Thank you to five very trusted and wonderful people who took precious time out of their busy lives to read my early manuscript and give me sincere feedback: my oldest daughter Kristina; my youngest daughter Adele; my close friend and mentor Betty; my dear friend Marilyn who is married to a Doukhobor man and lives in a Doukhobor community, therefore knows exactly where I'm coming from; and my good friend and pastor Rev. Dan. Each one of you has contributed important feedback in regards to specific and different aspects of this book. I was very insecure about publishing such a personal document, but each of you has encouraged me to do so. I, myself, have grown in understanding God's Word more clearly through the long process of writing. If this book helps even one person to realize that God loves them and encourages them to let Him be a part of their lives, it was well worth it.

Thank you to my beloved husband Tom, for being there for me and our daughters when we went through difficult times while raising our family. I also appreciate all your help with my computer issues while I was writing this book. You help me to keep a balance in my life, and I love the fun times we spend together travelling, camping, fishing, and kayaking.

Thank you to my sons-in-law, Marc and Darren, for enriching my life with your kind and caring personalities. Thank you to my five precious grandsons, Josh, Brody, Mathew, Brandon, and Adam for your contagious energy and enthusiasm for life. I am truly blessed and grateful to have each and every one of you enhancing our family.

Thank you to my older sister, Mildred for your help in remembering details of some events from our childhood days that are relevant to this book. It was interesting and fun to hash over memories from our youth as we tried to keep the facts straight. Thank you to my brother Rick for sharing with me your dream about the trees on our farm, and allowing me to use it here. Thank you to my brother Larry, and my sisters Laura and Ellen for all the family memories that we share. God in His wisdom has placed each one of you in my core family for a reason. Every single one of you is very spiritual, and could easily write your own book based on your own experiences.

Thank you to all the clergy, past and present, who minister to our little flock at the Logan Lake Christian Fellowship. Each one of you brings God's Word into our midst in your own unique way. We are truly blessed to have you leading our worship services every Sunday morning. Each one of you is a shining example of being Jesus' hands and feet here in our little corner of the world.

Thank you to all the beautiful people who have in the past, and still do today, attend the Logan Lake Christian Fellowship. You have been my one and only church family, and I am extremely blessed that God has placed me in your midst. It is here that I learned the importance of people gathering together to worship and praise God in a church. This is what keeps me grounded. Regardless of our denomination, our primary focus is on our loving God, Jesus Christ, and the Holy Spirit. I see God in each and every one of you, each in your own, special way. Many members have moved on to live in different locations, but pleasant memories of your time spent with us here always remain in my heart.

Thank you to each and every individual who has ever attended the weekly Bible Study meetings. Every single one of you has brought something specific and meaningful to our discussions. It is through our honest conversations and sharing here on Monday mornings that I learned that we all struggle with something. We have had many significant conversations and shared many laughs here. Your Bible based knowledge and attitudes towards both minor and major issues in today's world helps me to keep on track. I feel that each one of you is my sister or brother in Christ, and I am truly blessed by our conversations.

Thank you to our family friend from forever ago, Laura Veregin, for confirming my explanation about Doukhobors in the first chapter. I found it extremely difficult to try and sum up my entire cultural history in one short paragraph.

Thank you to all the individuals who have graciously given me permission to use your family's scenarios in this book. Each one of you has entered into my life at a crucial time of my spiritual growth. I am extremely thankful for your friendship. Without your individual stories, this book could not have been written.

All glory be to God.

ABOUT THE AUTHOR

Thelma has recently retired, and lives in the small mining community of Logan Lake, British Columbia with her husband.

She loves spending time with her family and friends, and travelling.

She has been actively involved in the local arts community as a painter, serves on the board of the Logan Lake Christian Fellowship, and enjoys soap making. Her hobbies include kayaking, going for long walks, cross-country skiing, snowshoeing, swimming, sewing, and reading.

Additional copies of this book may be purchased online:

Paper books at: www.Amazon.com

e-books at: https://www.smashwords.com/books/view/351428

Signed copies can be ordered directly from Thelma:

tfyuille@telus.net

*The farm south of Thunder Hill where I grew up. My grandmother
is on the path between the houses.*

My father playing the banjo for my daughters.

Me and my oldest daughter, Kristina,

shortly after the vehicle

accident.

Me and my youngest daughter, Adele, enjoying the day.

Me and Betty White, my mentor and my very dear friend.

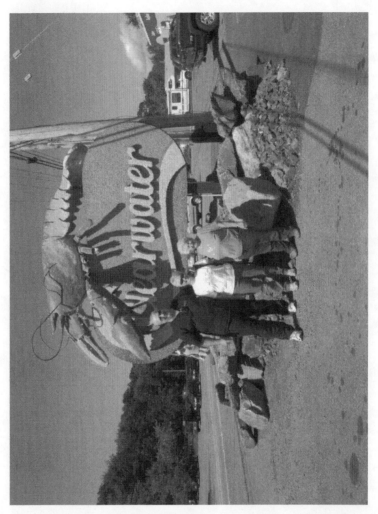

My husband Tom, me, and my mother on holidays in Nova Scotia.

Made in the USA
Charleston, SC
22 October 2014